OSWALD STREET

By
Vanesta Lewis

Published by:

Cover designed by Serena Rowe

Dedication

This book is dedicated to:
My husband Kenneth, who gave me permission
to tell our story;
Our four children, Kevern, Kendell, Kendrea, and
Kenneth, who lived the life we fashioned for them and
My family—my sisters and aunts—
who cushioned me through the challenging times.

Acknowledgement

Praise, honour, and adoration to my Heavenly Father, who never left my side even when I could not see Him.

I want to express my heartfelt thanks to all the women from the village whose indomitable spirits have nurtured me and whose voices I have become.

Greatest respect to Dr. Hilton Samuels; you have been an abiding friend. Thanks for listening.

Yasmin, you were there in school, always supporting me from those early years as primary school teachers, rushing to our wedding in that beautiful blue dress. I love you, my sister.

Shirley K, you left, but your laughter and voice remain. I am hoping to see you in paradise.

Elrose, thank you for your presence and honesty.

Special thanks to my editor, Hilette. I love your patience.

Mama, my story is your story. Dada, I wish you were here; you cared as only a father could.

Table of Contents

Introduction

After years of contemplation, I felt it was time. I felt an urgency to share my story. Its uniqueness lies in the fact that it is the story of the women who lived in the Village. I wanted to make it relevant. I wanted it to be a piece of the history of Streatham, both real and fictional. My story is the experience of many women. Women who have kept going simply because they needed to. In telling my story, I have given voice to these extraordinary women who lived and worked in that tiny village on Riley's Estate.

These women impacted my life in so many ways, and I could not have become the girl I was or the woman I am without them. Many of these women were denied the time, space, and opportunity to tell their stories. Many were uneducated, while some received minimum schooling and were in danger of being forgotten despite their sweat, tears, and faith.

It is out of this melting pot of strength, hardship, and love that I was born, raised, and began my journey into adulthood. On Oswald Street, I experienced joy, hope, and the desire to rebuild my life, my marriage, and, most importantly of all, my faith in God.

I hope that you will recognize the power of love, forgiveness, resilience, and peace with God as you read this book.

Chapter 1

The Village

The Village was located somewhere between the island's center and its eastern end. If you are unsure what that means, don't worry, I don't either. It was just *there*. It never seemed important; it was simply a part of Riley's Estate.

The soil was rich and fertile. Gentle rolling hills marked the southern end of the Village, but again, do not quote me as I still find it hard to find my way home if the bus stop changes. I would find it hard to navigate my way home now if there is so much as a change in the bus stop location. The soil was rich and fertile.

The Village was nestled at the foot of Windy Hill, aptly named for the constant winds that blew over, especially on those cold, foggy mornings in the wet season from September to

February. They were enough to chill the bones. In those days, the fog was so thick and deep that you could barely see a companion right next to you. As for the hill, it was so shrouded that the mist seemed impenetrable. It was like being enveloped in the arms of darkness. Yet, for all that eeriness, it was not at all threatening. In fact, it could be quite comforting.

The Village was not far from Dyers. Dyers lay possibly to the west where the closest grocery shop was. It was there that the youngsters on school holidays sometimes headed to buy saltfish, or other staples needed before the "grand" Saturday which generally took place in the capital. Too often, however, the basics needed would be in short supply at this tiny village shop, thus making the journey fruitless and frustrating. Furthermore, it was a lonely stretch of road at times, awakened only by the rustlings in the grass that lined the roadside.

Many are the stories told of the "jumbies" that haunted this lonely stretch of road. Besides, since those were the days when cars were few and pick-up trucks moved only during busy hours, travelling to Dyers was an excursion that never evoked excitement of any kind. Thus, it was that if you had an intrepid spirit, you could easily walk to Dyers in ten minutes flat. You just had to be bold enough (as a child) to walk past *Nineturning Ghaut* or *Nine Ghaut*. Tall trees brooded in frigid silence, watching with seemingly malevolent eyes as creaking limbs groaned menacingly, making the air glacial with fear. The scene was more than spooky. *It was terrifying.*

Of course, I was never fearful, or so I told myself. I just needed to walk briskly while constantly looking behind to catch a glimpse of what might have come out of the dense undergrowth or was peering eerily from either the mango or breadfruit trees that lined the ghaut like fearful sentinels. The sound of your heart thudding out of your chest was a sorry companion all the way down this tree-lined stretch until you were blessed by the sight of the three or four houses that stood on the promontory overlooking the main road.

Despite its mild horrors, the trek to Dyers during daylight hours was much more preferable than encountering the twists and turns that led past the burial ground en route to Harris, another neighboring village. Walking to Harris was quite a challenge. On the days when school was out, and you had to go to a shop in the centre of Harris to get flour, brown sugar, or rice, it was indeed a daunting task, certainly not suited for the faint-hearted. Thinking of rice (I digress), it was always filled with dry straw and even a few weevils. It had to be picked before washing, then cooked with pigeon peas, blue beans, or (in rare cases) black-eye peas.

It was lamentable that there were no real grocery shops in the Village. A makeshift shop provided rum, cigarettes, peanut-flavored sweets, mints, other hard candies, sweet biscuits, chewing gum, and *Phensic* tablets (a popular all-in-one pain and flu medication). The latter aside, these sought-after treats gobbled up the hard-earned pennies carried in the tightly-fisted hands of the village children who turned up frequently, eager to sample yet another coveted treat. Therefore, considering the rudimentary provisions of the local retail outlet, trusted little children would periodically need to get to Harris whenever the more substantial basics were needed.

To get to Harris, you first had to get over Farrells' Level, pass the back road leading into Windy Hill, then pass the brooding, two storied green house where the white ex-pat was said to have been buried. Shaking, sweating, and breathing hard from the exertion, you headed down the road toward the burial ground, keeping constant watch for snakes, frogs, or ground lizards—all of which posed an equal categorical danger.

The undergrowth was ever alive with unknown threats; being small, scared, and alone, you learned to walk away from the bushy roadside but more inclined to the right side of the road than walking in the middle. Twittering birds, rustling grass, and a thudding heart combined unwittingly to make doleful music as you crept by ravines, ghauts, and hillsides peppered with guava, turkey berry trees, and "Cheney" bush. Despite the energy expended, somehow, there was always enough remaining to enable one to sail past the enormous brooding mango trees looming overhead, ghost-like and silent over the steaming roadway— accelerated progress would not relent until you came upon the entrance to Paradise—peace *at last*.

Not so quickly though. The name Paradise was a misnomer since this farmland was shrouded in mystery and strange goings-on. This was where innocent little children were supposedly sent to meet "a man on a white horse" who "sold" them to the devil. Even though no one was ever "sold," the thought of this man on a white horse haunted many a gullible soul. Of course, not me. I was never scared, or so I told myself.

So, as life would have it, I walked to Harris on occasions when needed. I must admit that these occasions were relatively rare, as there was ample ground provision available so that we could comfortably wait for the weekly "rice treats" for Sunday dinner. While life in the Village was often hard, the sense of contentment, coupled with a desire to enjoy all they could from their lot in life, made the experience bearable and, for the most part, pleasant.

Chapter 2

Barefoot Disco

The Village was known for having quite an uncommon dance hall. People came from every corner of our island to mellow out in its modest environs, from Trench Town, Kinsale, George Street, Corkhill, and St. Johns. They came to revel, dance, and spree in the notorious Barefoot Disco. The main attraction was its band and, of course, the free-flowing liquor.

Barefoot Disco's band featured the Village's superstars and self-taught musicians. These musicians knew how to make their instruments hum, croon, or wail, depending on the mood of their avid listeners. Often, some minor squabble would erupt at the height of the fun. These eruptions didn't last long as the offending reveller was usually brought into submission or would exit the building under their own steam.

The "godly" older folks often viewed Barefoot as a den of vice. Village people were a weird combination of Christian morality and the spirit of bacchanalia. Sadly, possibly fortunately, this hotbed of fun and entertainment came by on the wings of opportunity and quickly flew by on the gales of confusion and strife. I can only speak of what I was told.

Often on weekends, the music and carousing would rage all night, Friday night, and again on Saturday night, but the occupants of the house on "the hill" could only tell that the party was in full swing from the music that blasted through the night. This was not an establishment they (the occupants on the hill) could visit or even consider visiting. It was a place for those who "no gat no Gad 'na dem" (have no God in them). It was a place of ill-repute, and they dared not even try to look in at the doors.

In fact, on one occasion, when one of the occupants dared to take herself to this "den of vice," her mama went to get her, much to her horror and mortification. Suffice it to say, none of the hill children ever attempted to darken the doors of Barefoot Disco again. They accepted that they should never enter such an iniquitous entertainment establishment.

This strange, forbidden house of entertainment was merely a garage built from corrugated iron with a concrete floor swept clean by a coconut broom. The music was unique since it was provided by a live band of local musicians whose skill with the guitar, uke, fife, drums, and shack-shack were almost a thing of legend. These self-taught musicians knew how to make those instruments throb with the beats of calypso, reggae, and other traditional sounds. "Allen and the Shooting Stars" was truly a band whose watchword was originality; they were definitely an orchestra to be reckoned with.

It was not only the music, culture, or noise that made this crude establishment memorable. The real fame and notoriety of that place came when, during a predicted hurricane, almost the entire village abandoned the relative safety of their homes to seek shelter from the howling winds and pounding rain within the precincts of its corrugated walls. Fortunately, the hurricane turned out not to be a full-blown powerhouse but a still formidable tropical depression. I highly doubt anyone had managed to sleep during the hours of that storm.

On the following day, long before sunrise, the occupants, along with their tiny bundles, all dreading the worst, sheepishly headed back to their small, wooden, galvanized, or thatched-roof houses. They were relieved to find them well intact, all safe and sound from the raging elements. The God of the winds had secured their dwellings. He knew these sharecroppers had no financial means to rebuild.

Barefoot Disco was such an anchor in the time of the storm, and thus, it attained legendary status. A few minor lifting of corrugated iron sheets showed that the losses could have been significant if there had been an actual hurricane, but thankfully, the damage was minor, and no one was hurt. The tale of this most unusual hurricane shelter became a reason for great jest as people across the little island heard with disbelief how a whole village population crammed into a corrugated iron garage to shelter from winds with tropical storm ferocity. No doubt, in the cramped conditions, some had huddled together, silently praying and pleading as the trembling roof desperately held through the night as the storm ravaged the valley.

When the Barefoot Disco was constructed, it represented an upgrade for the community. Before its existence, the village people enjoyed their own brand of entertainment, often in the form of penny concerts, which were held at the entrance to the Village. On such occasions, the creativity and imagination of the sophisticated thespians in the Village were at their best and most illustrious. Poetry, songs, and speeches dominated the stage as the performers made memorable deliveries, dressed in their "Sunday best," with legs shining (most times with petroleum jelly, coconut oil, or, on rare occasions, Jergen's body lotion).

Depending on the impact of their performances, participants were either paid to continue on the stage or removed for a mere penny amid the jeers and mocking laughter of the crowd. Then there were the more august occasions when men and women of stalwart speaking capacities eloquently delivered their "I hereby," "thereby," and "therefore" speeches. Indeed, these were colourful and illustrious occasions.

Sometimes, as these memories return to flood the mind and trigger spontaneous laughter or just a gentle smile, one can't help but wonder anew where these simple men and women had acquired the skill and knowledge to recite such long poems, to sing old hymns melodiously and in tune, croon beautiful ballads, or make a guitar, a fife or goat-skin drum resonate with such stirring, heartwarming tones. Despite their limited exposure to education beyond the early primary school years, being gifted and talented, their simple lives shone with life, fun, and laughter. So it was that on most Sundays, a concert atmosphere prevailed and found expression at the village entrance.

It would be careless not to mention the Sunday afternoon visits. Many villagers went to church on Sunday mornings and returned on a Sunday afternoon. As you walked past houses, the mouthwatering smell of fried fish, stewed chicken, beef, or mutton wafted by in the brightening glare of the afternoon sun. Somehow, the sun seemed brighter on Sundays than on any other weekday.

By four o'clock, the rounds began. Up the path came this noteworthy couple, hand in hand. Mister and Missis. Her hair was always well done, and her clothes were fashionable and brightly coloured.

He wore his hat, shirt tucked into his trousers, shoes polished and glistening in the afternoon sun. He held her in the crook of his arm as they strolled confidently, smiling on their journey to visit other couples of equal stature and dignity. It was as if they set the tone of all marital bliss as they smiled beatifically, sitting on the best chairs, and sipping whatever spirituous liquor was poured into the glasses that only came out of the cabinet for such auspicious occasions. These villagers had style and knew how to put on their brand of gentility. For years, this couple set a standard that was never to be replicated.

Marriage and divorce were never the topic of conversation or discussion. Quite a few couples just lived together. Some were single mothers, and some were widows. The ones who were married had long marriages. No matter what hit the families, whether infidelity, desertion, or even physical abuse, marriages remained. It may well be that the divorce of this trend-setting couple was the first of such bold steps in a community where it was not uncommon for two sets of children to grow up in two different homes but fathered by one astounding gentleman. This single divorce may well be linked to the change that was now taking place in the Village and, in fact, the island as a whole.

Chapter 3

Village Characters

One clear thing about the Village was that it was a closely knit community: everyone knew everyone else. Your business was everybody's business, and your grief was everybody's. All the children knew they were expected to respect all adults completely. Families were so closely interlinked that you had to avoid gross dishonour by "climbing up the horse's back to talk about its tail." You could never be sure how far back family ties and allegiances went.

If you were a stranger passing through or recently moved to the Village, you soon learned it was best to have as little as possible to say. It was often better to make peace or walk on by. Loyalties sometimes ran deep, but at other times, you would be compelled to wonder which doors loyalty had walked out through. Usually, when loyalty seemed to have temporarily slid underground, you knew the liquors had flowed too freely.

The rum shop was central to village life, and wherever a shop sprang up, you knew that liquor would be one of the available goods. Eventually, the three little shops in the Village sold almost everything needed: flour, rice, sugar, saltfish, onions, and various chicken parts. None needed fresh vegetables since almost everyone planted something.

Often, on a Friday afternoon, it would be possible to buy fried chicken and sweet potato pudding from the few vendors who covered their wares nicely under clean white towels and came to the roadside with their goods to make a few more pennies to supplement the family income. These were sometimes special investments to provide school uniforms and books throughout the school year.

Like every other village, this one was filled with its own theatre of colourful characters. It was impressive to watch the display, especially on Friday and Saturday afternoons when the rum flowed freely, and the surrounding hills and slopes were alive with the Reggae and Calypso that blared from the competing establishments, all within a three to five-minute walk of each other. These characters included the little man who would let it be known from the top of the hill overlooking the Village that when "womun come fan tong dem want to sh…" (when women come from town they want to poop).

Then, there was the one man who went to prison so often that he could repeat the prisoners' prayer with great confidence and triumphant hilarity.

"I love this place, O' God,

Where thieves and robbers dwell.

I just come to this beautiful motel,

Where thieves and robbers dwell."

This small-time conman made it his business to be sent to prison around Christmas time. He laughingly explains how he needed to be there to eat his share of the pig he had helped to raise, which was slaughtered for the prisoners' high-class Christmas dinner. A touch of wisdom must lie somewhere in this intricate argument.

Another man let everyone know that Friday was the devil's birthday. His words were often uttered with great glee. Having had his shower in the public bath, he dressed in his weekend regalia and headed off, never leaving the bar where he sat until the night was quiet. In the aftermath of his stay, his feet found their home purely by instinct.

The women were not to be outdone. One darling character was so inebriated that although quite unable to maintain the intended orientation, she would announce that she was going home straight (nonetheless swaying from side to side along the road, barely able to keep her balance). The truth behind her understanding of "straight" is that she would be stopping for no one. She knew when it was time to go, which was always about the time of sunset, and just as fast as it took the Friday afternoon sun to sink beneath the western horizon.

Music was in the very bones of the villagers. Reggae, Calypso, and ballads were often crooned with deep emotions, frequently bordering on despair. This dear woman usually wept as she sang, "Awinga wept, awinga wept. In the jungle, the quiet jungle, the lion sleeps tonight." Indeed, a strange lion prowled in the form of loneliness and deep-seated anxiety of more than a few villagers. Many did not have the language or the power to destroy the lion, and some died quietly at times, victims of the lion's grasp of alcohol and unexpressed disappointment.

There was no want of colourful characters. The Village was a veritable theatre. The creativity, ingenuous talents, and gifts of one family would have made some artists and designers of later years seem like novices. "Miss Goosey" came out every

Christmas. She was a replica of some aspects of the African traditions which made Caribbean Christmases so rich and colourful. Wooden stilts were made for the young man playing Miss Goosey to walk on. A female costume vibrant with colour reflected the spirit of carnival and dance. It was amazing to watch as this young man transformed into this terrifyingly tall creature, swaying to the music by which he was accompanied as he made his rounds through the Village. His brothers and friends strummed out the sounds of Christmas and carnival, paying homage to the ancestors and the spirit of Christmas. Although, as children, many of us were often scared, hiding behind skirts and dresses, many others both loved and feared Miss Goosey.

One could hear the banging of dominoes throughout the weekend, which was long with music and dancing, while some unfortunate worker squandered his week's pay with a deck of cards. This became so addictive for some that they never got up from around the domino table until the wee hours of Saturday morning, only to go home empty-handed. They would rest and prepare for another week of hard labour where the same behaviour would be repeated. While the losses were recounted with seeming indifference, none knew back then that this was called addiction. The impact on families went unnoticed. The failure to wisely use their meagre resources left many families in poverty. Broken and distressed, they faced a bleak future of lifelong addictions.

Some of the younger generation indeed acquired some of these habits. It was the change brought on by education, exposure by travel, and sheer determination that broke the back of many destructive and addictive behaviours. The late sixties and early seventies saw the seeds of change cascading through the Village. Still, much good came from the Village.

Addictive behaviours were so much a part of the Village life that they had become accepted as part of the fabric of family life. Children were the primary victims of this perpetuated cycle of poverty and hardship.

The church and schoolteachers understood little of the reality of the lives of the Village children and were so often harsh and critical of the meagreness of their lunches or the hand-me-downs they turned up in at school. Calico dresses, khaki shorts, and flip-flops were ordinary school wear. Many times, trousers were patched on top of patches, and dresses were worn until the material had become almost threadbare with age and whitened by repeated washings.

With the parents lacking any understanding of birth control, new children came regularly. Some teachers saw this as a reason to castigate children and make comments that drew the ire of the boldest and often more intelligent of the Village children. Some children left school, as they later said, because corporal punishment was ridiculous. Yet, for those who faced the enemy, the rewards were to prove life-changing. Change was approaching the Village, gaining gradual but steady momentum.

Chapter 4

The New Overseer

The winds of change were on the march, and the Village did not escape. Many of the villagers were still sharecroppers. The single shop in the Village was owned by the "overseer" who had replaced the white colonialists. Here was a bold figure with a massive personality and the tools to manipulate, control, and, in the process, garner a strange homage from the patrons of his establishment. The shop was his, the biggest one in all the villages. At some point, the only car in the Village was also his. The most fertile and accessible of the farmlands were in his grasp.

Having been overseas and accumulated experiences peculiar to the outside world, he had returned with great knowledge and resources. It was a natural progression (all agreed) that he would take up from where the colonialists had left off. As one kindly soul would note with awe and reverence, the man had returned from BG (British Guyana) an in a touch of altruism, he gifted all working-age residents with a gold chain. Such kindness was truly to be admired. The residents showed their deep appreciation with their commitment to work on the estate at minimum wage or whatever the going rate. His control of his willing subjects was admirable. The villagers were anchored in his service and thoroughly enjoyed it.

Being an entrepreneur with an eye for the next significant investment, he masterminded the Barefoot Disco. The allure of the simpler entertainments at the Village entrance soon died for want of spectators and participants alike. Our thespians no longer took to the stage to share their collective knowledge. After a full Saturday night of carousing and drinking, followed by church on Sunday morning, they were too tired to follow through with any other activity. The roadside theatre no longer echoed with laughter and goodwill on Sunday afternoons as everyone headed home to recuperate to meet the new week's challenges.

Change was on its way.

The old, corrugated garage that housed Barefoot Disco served a range of uses and functions throughout its lifetime. It was used as a storehouse for crops harvested from the fertile fields of Riley's Estate, Sunday School classes, and wonder of wonders, it even housed a church. The villagers knew how to make active use of space.

This building remains in the minds of those who knew it as a symbol of the metamorphosis of the Village. As the garage faded into insignificance, the Village slowly changed to adapt to the changing times.

Most of the villagers were subsistence farmers. Slave owners once owned the lands around this fertile valley. Sugar cane was cultivated, and its by-products, like sugar, strong rum, and molasses, were produced. By the 1960s, many of the villagers were sharecroppers. This meant they were given sections of the land to farm, but several rows belonged to the estate owner.

For many years, the estate was invariably run by our overseer, our returned resident traveller who had gone to BG. Even though he was still one of the villagers, many stood in awe of him, and he was afforded the revered title "Marse," which he accepted with great dignity as he exercised fearful control.

Other than his titled position of power, the distinctions he had made for himself—being one of the two individuals to own a car, owner of the only rum shop, and founder of the Barefoot

Disco—all served to accentuate his claim to power. His expansive entrepreneurial holdings also encompassed all the flat and arable land on the estate.

As a sharecropper, one was expected to allow the boss or one of his employees to take from the parcel of land whatever suited his fancy. They commonly took the biggest and best of anything to be harvested whenever the boss required it. It was not that gains from these were banked somewhere for the absentee landlord; it was just that the boss could take it, so he did. Rents for the land were later paid to the overseer, and each worker on the estate had a little rent book that recorded the amount paid and the date.

The difference between attitudes to education and the basic ability to read and write became evident when it was later revealed that this business manager had no formal education and could not read. It did make sense when it became apparent that the resident overlord intended to prevent the "serfs" from educating their offspring. By the early fifties into the sixties, more and more parents recognized the power of educating their children. Even though some parents could barely read, they were intent on sending their offspring to school. The government began taking control of the church schools, saving the upcoming generation from a life of penury.

The influence of the overseer waned in significance as he was forced to depend on his rum shop more and more. The rise of new ambitious politicians in the region was part of this change, as they attempted to wean the people from their dependence on sharecropping.

Chapter 5
Community Strength

To get work done and make a living from the land without a large outlay of capital, the villagers often resorted to what was known as "murroons." This was when one farmer would invite others to help with a substantial piece of work while the wife and other village women would cook food for the workers. Food was quite plentiful on these occasions, and the white rum or Mount Gay rum flowed freely. These murroons were occasions of hard work but also brought great merriment and goodwill. The men would bank (make rows in) the soil in preparation for planting while some women planted. Sometimes, especially when sweet potato vines were being planted, it was the children who dropped them on the banked soil. Work would begin quite early in the morning before the sun was too high in the sky.

Food was cooked on a wood fire in large tins, the staple being breadfruit, dasheen, yams, sweet potato, or whatever root crop was in season, and there were usually dumplings (a mixture of flour, salt, oil, and sometimes other ingredients to add flavour and variety), the highlight of any meal. Coconut, corn meal, "musha" (dried cassava meal), or even sweet potato were also added to the flour to create something hearty and filling. Everyone who turned up was fed. The work was often completed in record time. Sometimes, these murroons were held in the afternoons as some who needed this help would have gone to earn some money at a day job. Some hired out themselves to work for someone else who could pay for a couple of days of labour.

Whenever it was time for the "man-in-charge" (the overseer) to hold a murroon, all the world came to support him. It was like a carnival in his fields. He would arrive in his car to stand and watch as he loudly chatted to all who would hear (usually followed by his chosen entourage of minute men who hung on to his every word and acted out his commands even before they left his mouth). But in the style of true "Massa," he never really dirtied his hands with the menial tasks being carried out for his little plantation. No one seemed to find it odd that everyone worked at other murroons except him. They all easily bought into the concept that this was how things must work.

Sometimes, a family might need to move a house they had bought or inherited to a different place in the village. These wooden structures were loaded onto a tractor and transported to its new foundations on such occasions. Those were days when houses were built on nags, and all the men would be on hand to lift the house using wood logs and simple tools. Once the house was settled onto the tractor, sometimes the men would settle themselves inside it or on the side of the tractor to ensure they were on the spot in time to unload it from the tractor.

It was out of this collage of fun, hard work, feuds, and community-building spirit that children born in the changing fifties were thrust upon the world to foster the change and tenor of village life.

Chapter 6

Dark Days

Many women were the heroes and mainstay of the lives of their children. The women were the first to grab hold of the idea that education was the avenue for change. They knew that the highly unregulated activity of sharecropping was detrimental to their plans for educating their children. Many were afraid to challenge the system, and it made the few who wanted to break the yoke feel they were stepping above their station. It was thought that they should keep their heads down and, when needed, send their older children out in the fields to work the "toss" (that is, to help them work on the allotted section of the fields they had to cover by the end of the day).

Education impeded the quick shilling or the much-needed dollar. Yet, payments were decidedly low. The hours were long, and life was hard. It was my cousin, who, as he fought to restrain his anger, shared with me the penurious wages they were paid for working their toss. He noted that in the days of his grandmother (around the first decade of the 20th century), it was as little as six pence per day, which moved to one shilling, then to a shilling and sixpence until it became the vast two and six. The price paid for keeping bright young minds in low-skilled jobs was not to educate them. Enslaving them meant resisting the winds of change.

As the estates began to lose more workers, marginal attempts were made to pay a little more to end and weaken the stranglehold of poverty. No one outside these villages seemed to be able to do anything. It was left to the landowner to determine what was paid. But it was becoming more apparent that change was on its way. By the time I could remember and understand, it had gone up to seven dollars a day in the mid-sixties. One could then understand why sometimes some children were awakened before the cock crowed to help their mothers work the toss. They then left in time to get to school by nine o'clock. It seems this was the age of strange indifference.

Even though many of the teachers in the one-room schoolhouses came out of this stark poverty, they felt it a masterful duty to increase the tiredness and suffering of any tardy pupil. It was well known that anyone who arrived after nine was met with a strap; hence, no one wanted to be late. Children learned how to run down those hills, corners, and gullies to make it to school before the bell rang.

It was this worthy son, my cousin (John Whoopsie), who spoke with barely concealed anger of his refusal to go into the fields of the new overseer to work. The cultural beliefs and ancestral practices made these young men refuse to be tied down. It was clear to him that those who worked in these fields were unable to break free of the enslavement and treachery ingrained in estate labour. Many believed that once anyone entered these fields, they could not get out. They were trapped. To escape this trap, some learned skilled trades, and where they could brave the unknown, they travelled to Great Britain (the mother country), where they were taught by their misguided, deceived educators to make a life for themselves.

For many, their dreams descended into madness. They soon came to appreciate that back home, reclining under the swaying of the coconut tree or stretching dangerously out on a limb to pick ripe breadfruit was a taste of heaven. The fierce racism they met sent some right over the brink. The struggles they faced were harrowing and traumatic. That, however, is another story. Suffice it to say their ability to fight back in the face of tremendous odds is captured in the fact that many of them lived well into their eighties and nineties. Change had to come.

The Trade Winds swept their way onto the island, and the mothers born in the 1920's were determined to educate their children. This spirit of determination and independence would sustain and impact the lives of the children who issued forth and learned to excel amid these turbulent and interesting times.

Chapter 7

Religious Rest

Despite the struggles, the villagers were all quite religious. On a Sunday morning, many families or parents would take a walk up to the Anglican Church in Harris, where they would solemnly sit and listen to the "Father" (priest), partake of holy communion, greet each other, and then head off to the grocery-cum-rum shop.

This was where children bought sweets, chewing gum, sodas, and sweet biscuits while the older folks had their draught of one of the fiery spirits on offer. In fact, on most occasions, the women headed home to prepare the Sunday dinner, while the men went from shop to shop or from house to house, where they continued to imbibe until late into the afternoon and evening. It was amusing to watch them rolling home with their "jackets" slung over their shoulders, calling good night to each other.

Every Sunday morning, without fail, as the sun rose over the hills, shedding its brilliance on the gently rolling fields and hillsides, a sense of deep peace descended over the entire village. From every home, transistor radios pounded out songs by Jim Reeves, George Beverly Shea, Andre Crouch, and others, giving praise and thanks to God. Radio Paradise was the one to listen to on a Sunday. Yes, it was true; the villagers were indeed quite religious.

These songs often carried a moralistic tone, and one of my favourites reminded and pleaded with the alcohol vendor, "Please don't sell Daddy any more whiskey." This one was a Sunday afternoon special. Ironically, when this reverberated on the hills and valleys, the white rum and Mount Gay rum flowed freely in the tiny bars and rum shops.

Village life was filled with chaos, dreams deferred, hope, and hard work. Many voices screamed silently into the night air. In the ploughed and forked furrows of the land, many were lost in the din and battle for survival, with stories left untold and tears unshed.

Sunday was the day to recuperate and prepare for the challenging week ahead. On Sunday, the school clothes were ironed, homework was done, and the best meal of the week was cooked and eaten. By sunset Sunday evening, the road was quiet. The drinkers had retired to sleep off the booze, and a restful quiet covered the house with blobs of light here and there marking where the houses were.

By cock crow on Monday morning, no matter how hard they had drank or how long they had sat at the domino tables, the men were off to work, and women were busy getting the water and lighting up the fires to make breakfast. The older children would be out alongside their parents, doing their share of the household chores. By eight o'clock, the roads were alive with the sound of laughter and the smell of fried or roasted breakfast. The motivation continued to shift as each new week began, another step on the ladder of reformation and development.

Chapter 8

Village Life

Since the villagers were sharecroppers, the "Big Man" would send his collectors to get his share from the estate workers at specific points during the harvesting season. Some meekly gave up what was demanded, but others, like my mother, kicked against the injustices of this system. On several occasions, she chased the men out of her field, and on one occasion, she threatened to do the Big Man himself bodily harm if he set foot in her garden. She planted herself firmly within one of the banks, armed with her cutlass and with the determined spirit of a warrior queen, while she found several choice epithets to describe him.

My father, who was sick, weakly called to my mother to let them have the bunch of bananas they came to take, but she stood her ground. This lone ranger had already allocated the proceeds from the sale of this bunch of bananas to purchase our clothing for school, and she did not back down. Having encountered her warrior-like spirit on previous occasions, the Big Man and his collectors eventually backed off. Never again did any of them attempt to set foot on the land on which she laboured tirelessly. From long before sunrise until midday, she worked and then came home to cook, clean, and wash our clothes, having sent us off to school to get an education.

Times were often challenging, but life had to be lived. My mother was determined that we had to go to school. The story of my village is a story of many other villages on our small island home. These early experiences molded us into the men and women we would become.

Could anything good come from the Village? Poverty stalked us like a plague. Often, as our mother worked and sang, she would sometimes sigh, "Aye sah, poorness of life." Then she would burst into laughter. These women knew how to cope. Despite their hard work, they often could only provide the basics or just enough, as some would say, to "keep soul and body together." There was barely enough ready cash to buy the necessities. These were the days when the shopkeeper wrote in a book what you purchased, and payments were made at the end of each week. These were the days when parents had to save to buy school clothes. Children knew their church, school, and house clothes were different. It was pretty common to have one pair of shoes for church and one for school, and for the rest of the time, you either played barefoot around the yard or you wore a pair of rubber slippers or maybe an old "soft walker" which could no longer be worn to school.

Practically every family subsisted on the land. Children learned early how to weed carrots, plant vines, pick peas, and tend the animals kept for food to supplement their meagre income in the festive season. Now and then, a sheep would be butchered. Some were held for that special family feast day, and others were kept for sale to a city butcher or the neighbour.

Chapter 9

Market Day

On Saturdays, the women packed what they had reaped and headed to the public market in the city to hawk their vegetables. On these days, the women all dressed in their clean and well-pressed market dresses went into the city. Those who were handy enough would have their aprons ready to tie over their dresses to avoid the stains from sweet potato or green banana. Heads were wrapped in colourful head ties, some worn at rakish angles to reflect their love of dressing up and their skill at making the most of what they had.

The women all travelled together on the backs of pick-up trucks. Their goods were packed into baskets and crocus bags, while the more delicate produce, such as tomatoes, ripe bananas, and Julie mangoes, were carried in trays or plastic containers. They set off for the day with much laughter and goodwill and returned in the evenings, having sold as much of their goods as possible. They would return with cooking oil, salt fish, mackerel, rice, flour, pig's tail/snout, fresh beef fish, chicken back, and a whole chicken for the elite few. These were some of the staples that were not readily available at the village shops. Besides, they were much cheaper in town.

Strange was the attitude of the men. Very few of them would decide to stand in the market and sell their produce. That was a woman's work. Even in preparing the land for planting, there was an unwritten, unspoken law that women did not fork the ground; that was for men. Yet among them were the few "Amazon women" who stood head and shoulders with the men in the heat of the day. In a very real way, there was "women work" and "men work." Very few men would take up the responsibility to go and sell vegetables in the public market. The market was for women.

The villagers worked hard, but they also played hard, and often, the sounds of cursing, swearing, and fighting disturbed the beautiful tranquility of this lush green valley, especially on the weekends. People spoke louder, drank more heavily, and sometimes beat the wives who had dared to demand money to supplement what was earned from hawking their produce. The Village was caught in a time loop from which it could not escape. They seemed doomed to work, play, get old, and wait for the "Lord to take them." Through all this turmoil, however, it was still possible to see the hope for change in the Village.

A lone preacher established his church in the Village, its open doors pleading with the residents to come in. Very few attended. Some, loyal to their familiar brand of religious zeal, still headed off on Sundays to the Anglican Church in Harris, and a few attended the Pentecostal church in Dyers. Many Sundays, this faithful voice sang and preached to the empty seats in his church. A few children sometimes stepped inside, and one or two older folks. I do not think they trusted the idea of a church outside of the norm, a church not linked to the traditional churches. Eventually, this voice gave way to an established church, with its members seeking to garner more lost souls into its precincts.

It was much quieter on Sundays in the late seventies and into the eighties. More families stayed indoors, and the drinking and brawling in many families subsided. The children of the late fifties and early sixties were moving away from the meagreness of life in the shadows of sharecropping.

Chapter *10*

Hopes for the Future

Amid all this, many were bent on preparing their children to find a better way. Many taught their children that earning their living with a hoe and fork was a disgrace. For them, this was the pathway to poverty, slaving in the hot sun daily to eke out an existence. Children had to go to school and learn trades. Some were apprenticed to seamstresses and carpenters. Sadly, some of these skilled artisans were often not honest about how they trained or remunerated their apprentices. It was going to be left to the children of the up-and-coming generation to change the face of the Village.

Education was never the priority of many grandparents. Children living with them were often kept out of school to look after younger siblings or to pick cotton during the season. A few escaped the harshness of poverty, putting together what money they could and migrating to other islands in the Caribbean or as far away as Panama to work on the Panama Canal. Very few ever returned or were heard of again. Some later went to the mother country as part of the Windrush generation. Their lives were difficult. Very few of those left behind knew the extent of the alienation they experienced and the hardships they faced. It was only in the twentieth century, when a volcano erupted, forcing the relocation of many, that the children, nieces, and nephews whose hopes nestled in some far-off sands understood the cruelty and discrimination experienced by these brave souls and why some of them came back with "snow" in their brains. Heartbreaking as it was, that story cannot be told here.

For many older folks born in the first decades of the twentieth century, the only world outside the Village was Plymouth, commonly referred to as the city or town. These simple people worked the same lands their parents worked, learned the trades their parents passed on to them and lived only to put food in the mouths of their offspring. They ensured that the children had at least one good suit to wear to the doctor in case they got sick and, in some cases, one or two suits to wear to church on Sunday. Believers, after their sort, were convinced children had to be christened (baptized), and while they may not regularly attend throughout the year, they made that grand effort to turn up at church on special days such as Easter Sunday, Christmas, and the New Year. Indeed, these were occasions to be witnessed mainly for the dress-up parade.

Businesses such as Charles Mercer and O.R. Kelsick enjoyed a booming business on the days leading up to these special Sundays. Hardly anyone ever bought ready-made dresses. The local seamstresses would make these fine dresses after the materials had been obtained from the merchants mentioned above. The colours were bold and vibrant, yet subtle. These simple women knew how to choose the finest, and their simple means would allow them to purchase. As the years brought enlightenment, these local masterpieces were replaced with store-bought dresses, or some transported from England and America or islands such as Curacao and the American Virgin Islands. These, however, never equalled the creativity and finesse of the locally produced dresses. But the Village women saw the ability to buy a store-bought dress as a step on the rung of modernity. So, they acquiesced. The dresses from England never really took off, as they often fell far short of beauty and boldness. They came in trunks and parcels, but very few were suited to our island home's sweltering warmth.

These simple, strong, resilient women had style and a strange sense of pride. Quite a few were still unable to read, but they could sense that change was coming. They did not always understand it or have the language to voice their fears and struggles. However, they quickly accepted the idea that a choice was available to them. They valued democracy after their fashion. General elections in the burgeoning era of the late, much-loved statesman William Bramble brought them a sense of pride. Election time was a time of celebration. At times, they may not have understood the real issues, but they knew they owned the land their parents had squatted on, so they made their "X" with solemn dignity.

Chapter 11

Home and Family

It is sometimes difficult to define what a family is. By Village standards, a family is deemed as a group of people living in the same house. Family is also the extended circle of aunts, uncles, cousins, grandparents, and in-laws that have a part in shaping who an individual would become. In those days, we had in the family some brave souls who had escaped to other islands, the mother country, Panama, and America, to help relieve the austere conditions of home.

We were the family on the hill living on the borders at what was facetiously called Oswald Street. At home, we had the constant presence of mother and father. However, by whatever mysterious series of circumstances, another entire family lived across the way, around the corner on the farther side of the Village who were also our siblings. We were children growing up together. My blood siblings and I attended the same school; some of us were in the same class as our half-brothers and sisters. Maybe this would have been a time to develop a healthy and powerful clan, except the adults who created the fraternity never encouraged or fostered the brotherhood that could have shaped the lives of the innocents involved. Rather than encouraging bonding, there was bitter enmity, rivalry, and ardent dislike. There was one man but three women and three sets of children. How were we ever to intermingle and be content? We existed, avoided each other, and were "cut-eyes" (looking with disdain and making angry faces at each other).

In my home, I was the fourth and middle child of the lot. As times were so hard at different times, one or another of my half-siblings lived with us for short periods. While the women actively disliked each other, as children, we could cut eyes at our half-siblings but had no authority to be disrespectful to their mothers. When they came, our mother ensured that all were treated with equity.

My three older siblings were hardier than I was, and even though I could do my share of the household chores, I was often sick. As children, we were not allowed to sleep late, beyond the sun's rise. We were up early to collect the day's water, sweep the yard, and lead the domestic animals to the pasture.

We were generally up by 6 a.m. The bedding was put away, and the room was cleared and ready for daytime use. We did not always agree; we were always reluctant to embrace these early mornings, especially in the rainy season when the mornings were cold and the fog sat on Windy Hill, keeping its baleful eye in the valley. We crossed over, and we kept going. We knew one thing for sure—we were loved.

By 1972, there were seven of us at home: two brothers and five sisters. My mother had lost two babies in the process, and my oldest sister, Mama's oldest child, died as a little girl from possible pneumonia, but the older people in the village insisted it was a "jumbie" that killed her. My mother, never one to embrace superstition, insisted it must have been pneumonia; the unavailability of doctors in the late forties rendered a proper diagnosis impossible.

At first, our home on the hill was a tiny two-roomed house. It eventually became a bit larger when an aunt who had braved the cold of the mother country felt it was time to return to the island for a much-needed holiday. She helped my parents add another two rooms. We were happy despite the limited availability of most of the world's luxuries and extravagant resources, which were within easy reach of professionals and entrepreneurs.

We, the children, knew that during the school holidays, we would have to help weed carrots, sweet potato vines, or whatever crop our parents planted. We found ways to enjoy our "labour." For instance, when we had to carry the dung to manure the fields, we would race to see who could get to the fields first. On occasions when we had to plant the dried corn kernels and blue beans, we would compete along the long rows until, in the heat of the mid-morning sun, our energy would wane, and instead of two seeds in each hole, we would chuck handfuls. Our father would remind my brother and me that the seeds could talk when he came back with empty containers. We soon understood why when they started to grow.

Our father would question us when he came home and ask if we had done as he asked. Of course, we would brightly respond "yes," only to be told, "de two a you a some damn bad pickney." Thus, we were punished simply by the tiredness in his voice. Despite all we had to do, carry water, help in the "ground," keep the house and yard clean, water the cows, and take and bring home the sheep, we were happy most of the time.

Chapter 12

The Making of
the Parents

Sadly, not everyone was quick to sail on the winds of these early changes. Some were fearful that going off to study reading and writing would deprive them of their immediate cash flow. Therefore, even though church schools were established, some parents did not see the value of educating their children, while others felt they simply could not afford to send their children to school.

My mother, being the eldest child in the house, was educated up to third standard. This meant that formal education for her had ended when she was about ten years old. Her attendance at school during those five years was often erratic, as during the cotton-picking season, she had to take the donkey down to Farms to bring home the cotton her parents had picked.

In addition, there were some days when it was simply impossible for her to attend. She had to stay home to help with looking after her younger siblings while our grandmother went off to work her toss on the estate (which was sometimes as far away as Farms Village). After such arduous days of labouring, she would still come home to attend to her own patch of ground around the four-roomed house which housed a family of eleven. My mother spoke of this with hardly any resentment. She understood my grandparents' choices, even though she disagreed with the approach.

Consequently, Mama's school days were curtailed as she learned to shoulder her share of family responsibility (which was not hers rightfully). Years later, she recalled how when she had to pass the school on her way home from Farms with the cotton on the donkey, her class teacher would come out to berate her for not attending school. She would dig her heels into the sides of the donkey, which was a sign for it to "kick up" (this meant kicking up its back legs so that whoever was unfortunate enough to be within reach would get a solid blow from the donkey) forward, thereby escaping her episode of shame and disgrace. She knew enough to defend herself so no one could make a fool of her. Over the years, she became more proficient, as we had to read aloud so she could hear as we sat around the oil lamp doing our homework at night.

My mother had a fantastic memory. She loved to repeat poetry and often repeated some of the verses she had learned in her short stint at school. One of her favourites was *Lord Ullin's Daughter* by Thomas Campbell. She also learned the Psalms and many songs and ballads. Often, as she laboured in our yard, house, or fields, she would sing them.

Mama knew she could not help us with algebra and geometry, which seemed to be the bane of every child's life. The unfortunate village teacher—who had fallen victim to "obeah" (witchcraft), leading to the loss of his job at the government-run school—helped my older siblings with those challenging arithmetic problems. These arithmetic problems were the kinds that must have been issued from the mind of some rebel genius who hated young learners. Never again, in our later years, did we encounter such meaningless and complex word problems. In exchange for dinner, ground provisions, or whatever vegetables my mother could afford, he helped my siblings with the arithmetic homework.

My father fared much better. He was sent to school, except for those times he missed due to illness. Those were the years when "chiga" was popular, and when one came under the attack of these parasites, the victim could not walk until they were picked out from the soles of the feet or between the toes of the unfortunate host. These parasitic mites, the product of dirty water and poor drainage systems, would burrow their way into the feet of the hapless victim, where they reproduced, causing extreme pain and swelling. Parents became adept at treating them, and eventually, with a clearer understanding of proper drainage and better hygiene, they just disappeared. For some time, my father was a victim of these vicious creatures and had to stay out of school. When these creatures were embedded in their feet, walking was impossible, much less putting shoes on one's feet.

My father often recalls how his parents had more than they needed. Hospitality was the most natural thing to happen throughout the community, and usually when a neighbour or visitor passed by, they were expected to stay for dinner. No matter how simple the food was, there was always enough to share. My grandparents went to the next step. They would simply pack bags with vegetables and send my father or one of his siblings to take them to some family they suspected was in need. This spirit of care and concern was so widespread that people would put their pots on ready to cook, knowing that food would be supplied.

Another common practice was sending children to live with relatives or godparents who were either alone or getting on in years. So, my father moved away from home to live with his godparents, whose children had moved to another Caribbean Island. They ensured he was sent to school, which was not always the case in these situations. Living with them, he went to school regularly and wore shoes and socks.

Dada had a deep love for reading and books. Our two-roomed house on the hill always had books, and whenever the Jehovah's Witnesses or the Seventh-day Adventist colporteurs came by, my father would buy one or two of their books.

One of the most powerful and lasting images of my father is of him sitting in the cool evening with the huge family Bible he had bought from the colporteurs in his hand, reading until the sun had set. My father was a singer with a beautiful voice, and often, during his later years, he sang the "Songs of Zion," as we called them. Mama sang, too, but she often admitted that she could not "cut a tune" like Dada. She had one skill he lacked: he could not dance. She would laughingly say he had two left feet, which I believe I have inherited.

Mama and Dada complimented each other in many ways. Mama loved to laugh and was quite astute. Dada was much quieter than her. He was hard-working, kind, and helpful, but he did not have the analytical mind that enabled Mama to readily spot weak or unscrupulous characters.

Chapter 13

Our House on
the Hill

With four children, me being the baby, my parents moved into our tiny two-roomed house on the hill. In those days, the whole Village came to help move tiny wooden structures to the piece of land villagers were allowed to squat on. While most of the houses lay in the valley below us, it seems we were set as a city that couldn't be hidden.

Our neighbours were two older women whose children had already grown up and moved away to more prosperous Caribbean islands or the United Kingdom. Fields of guava backed our tiny house in an area known locally as Diamond. Not far away was Dannenborg Farm, owned by white expats, a spillover from the days of sugar cane.

The rough dirt road that was to become Oswald Street was dominated by a tower, another replica of the sugar days. Mama had been peremptorily discharged from her parents' home, and here is where she settled.

We lived on the hill; we grew up on Oswald Street. We did not know it then, but this was *our* street. It nestled in almost silent dignity just below the tower, across from the cistern. It was a place that was sometimes believed to be haunted, possibly linked to the fact that our garden was filled with giant trees and electricity had not yet reached the hill. The tiny lights that flickered through the trees from the three houses on the hill were felt to be the lights of "jumbies" or, in some far-fetched tales, "jack-o-lanterns."

I must admit that I was often scared when the sun had set, and the darkness settled over the village with a meagre light from the oil lamps or few streetlights on the road in the valley. Sometimes, on a Sunday afternoon and rarely during the weekdays, we would visit our grandmother, who lived in the valley below us. At night, the roads would be peppered with frogs hopping wherever they were to spend the night. I was terrified of anything that hopped, crawled, or rustled. I would usually try to get home before these creatures invaded the narrow track leading up the hill.

Sometimes, I failed to leave on time, and whenever my mother looked out and saw me standing in the road, she instantly knew the problem. My older brother would have to come and get me. I stood there watching the frog sitting in the path as if listening and waiting for instructions. It did not move, and I could not move either. My brother was none too pleased on such occasions, but he knew we had to look out for each other.

Oswald Street was established in 1980 when the government cut a new road to replace the dirt road that connected Streatham (The Village) and Windy Hill. It was the young Rasta man who moved into the tower and made it his home who etched his name into the street, and thus we adopted the name as fitting since he was the only one from the valley below who ever considered residing on the hill. Years later, when my young husband and I built our house on Oswald Street, we planted passion fruit over the cistern. Passion fruit was a fitting symbol of our tempestuous marriage. I will tell you about us later, but as the old saying goes, "It takes two to tango."

Chapter 14

Growing up on Oswald Street

I told you my life in the Village was diverse and wonderful. My parents loved and took care of us. As I mentioned before, my father raised two other families alongside ours. He eventually married my mother, but I have siblings born to the two other women either in the same year or within a year of each other.

We were altogether fifteen siblings, not counting the ones that had died at birth or in early childhood. I learned how to live and share in a large family. I learned how to avoid conflict with silence. I learned how to act superior and forgive when it suited me. I learned how to be angry and suppress my anger. But I also knew what love, hard work, dedication, and patience looked like. Weird. Strange. The human psyche is resilient, malleable, and beautiful.

My parents took us to church on a Sunday (in the days before we became Seventh-day Adventists) when they could afford to. My three older siblings and I were encouraged to be "confirmed" (become official members of the Anglican church). We went to the confirmation class, and we were all confirmed. This was all a part of the religiosity of the community. At some point, everyone went to church. My father read the Bible, and we heard and learned Christian songs, many of them at Sunday school. Sunday school was a must for village children, and we loved it. It was run by a lady from the Pentecostal church every Sunday in the shadow of the garage (later known as Barefoot Disco).

Feet washed and in the neatest house clothes we possessed, village children hurried off as soon as we saw Sister Mainie stroll towards the meeting place. Sister Mainie was our favourite respectable and kind adult. She held a special place in our hearts.

I enjoyed learning the memory gems and singing, especially "Jesus loves me this I know" and "Happiness is to know the Saviour." A few families never attended church, but for the rest of us children, Sunday school was where we learned about

God. It brought all of us village children together, and we learned values and principles we wouldn't have had access to had it not been for such a refreshingly simple environment.

Sunday school had special treats—bread and cheese with a sweet drink. It was nothing spectacular, but it was just simply special and memorable. After Sunday school, children often hung around and loitered in the street until sunset, even though we were never allowed to. As soon as Sunday school ended, we knew we should be heading home.

Sometimes, we lingered, looking longingly for any distraction that could prolong our time together. When we did not get home promptly, our mother stood on the hill and called to us. While we could participate freely in the learning experiences, socializing was carefully monitored and curtailed. Mama did not believe children should be given such free rein. I understood how the complicated family structure made her so careful of where we were and who we were with. This watchfulness was to impact my life in significant ways. Life in a protective, reactive, compelling village was filled with twists and turns, stifling and restless, and at times as serene as the gently rolling hills and verdant valleys; nothing is ever what it seems.

Our father rarely issued corporal punishment; thinking about it, Dada never really spoke. We were close to him by being far. We clearly understood what we were expected to do, but as the years went by, we knew he had expectations that he never voiced. Perhaps he did not have the words, and maybe he just thought we knew. Much of the disciplining was left to our mother, who clearly wanted something better for us, and she hammered her expectations into our minds in the simple ways she knew how.

In my early years, they argued and fought quite often. They were fine when there were no outside influences and would speak long into the night, deciding what would be planted and whether they had to slaughter one of the animals to provide meat for the upcoming days. It was evident that our father recognized he had a strong and good wife, but when he stayed too long at the bottle or waited too long at the rum shop, they had bitter conflicts.

Mama was determined, ambitious, and confident in herself and what she wanted for her children. She could not be silent about what she called Dada's recklessness, his kindness that allowed others to benefit at his expense. She would tell him with unshakeable clarity, and he would seek to assert his authority by hitting my mother. He would get drunk and spend his week's pay, leaving nothing to depend on besides what was planted on the plots of land they farmed together.

The quiet peace on the hill would often erupt into angry words, bitter recriminations, and terror would reign. Weekends were the time for these blasts of anger and screaming. He did not hit her often because my mother was fearless, and she did not back down. We all hated these horrific showdowns, yet we were never physically abused. We wept silently sometimes as the alcohol-fueled feud burned late into the night. Gradually, the embers would die, and all you would hear was, "A know. These bones could keep," (I will survive), and then a dead silence would descend on the house. It was as if an unseen hand had clamped lips together; they would both go quiet, and peace would return. Then, the winds seemed to caress the galvanized roof, crickets tweeted in the grass, and frogs croaked in the pond at the back of our little house on the hill.

By the next day, my father would be the epitome of quiet, dignified silence. It is as if he was so ashamed he would barely speak. Sometimes, he would need to work at six in the morning. Mama would get out of bed, cook if required, pack his lunch bag, and have his tea ready when he returned from "shifting" (moving) the animals and milking the cow. Not once, as far back as I can remember, did she fail to ensure he was well-presented and fed.

Eventually, as we grew up, Dada recognized the folly of what had been happening; he now toned down his undesirable behaviours. He continued to work hard and spend more time at home, but now he put aside the liquor. Change had come. The winds that fanned the flames of strife subsided, and the fires that had flared in the many tumultuous confrontations on Oswald Street smouldered and burnt themselves out as we matured into adulthood. A powerful metamorphosis had begun.

Today, the liberated woman would ask why her mother never thought of leaving my father to his vices and going it alone. I had asked her once. Her answer was simple and filled with a strange truth: loyalty. She told me, "He is your father." She meant, "I have to take care of you and him." Strange. My father told me in his later years. "I never thought I have ever seen a prettier woman than your mother. I would be up a tree if I had listened to her." Meaning he would have been more successful in life. They somehow had a conception of commitment that defies the modern enlightened psyche.

Chapter 15

The children of Oswald Street

Work and industry were important to our parents. We had to learn to do chores or "help out" in and around the house and on the farmland. Overlooking the Village were the lush hillsides, some with steep slopes, others gently rolling and covered with produce, and the sweat and hard work of many Village folk. Sweet potatoes, carrots, corn, tomatoes, and pigeon peas were just a few staples that flourished on the rich, dark soil on these slopes.

In some of the ravines and ghauts on Riley's mountains, my parents kept animals to sell as meat during the festive seasons. They also kept chickens to provide the eggs and meat. Rather than being kept in a coop, these domestic birds freely strayed and fed around the yard, making the mango, avocado, and cedar trees surrounding our home their nightly abode.

Early in the morning, long before the break of day, the roosters would begin to crow. As we grew older, we learned to recognize that this sound meant you had a few more hours before you had to get up and begin chores. As soon as it was light enough, my older brother and sister headed out with the sheep, taking them out to pasture in fields around the area my father farmed. The chickens clucked around the yard, and they too had to be fed at times to keep them 'tame,' as they were free to scratch for worms, and would at times target seeds in the garden around the house, and that was if there were no peas blossoms for them to destroy.

Some of us headed off to the standpipe at the foot of the hill to fetch the water Mama would need for washing and cooking when she returned from the fields. She would do these chores after she had sent us off to school. Sometimes, especially between December and January, the mornings were cold, and the hill overlooking Oswald Street would be covered in dense fog, the grass smothered in dew, and the wind rushed over the hill, causing one's teeth to rattle. On such chilly mornings, we would be wrapped in old sweaters, jackets, or whatever insulating outer garment that could be found to keep the bite of the wind from penetrating thin cotton dresses, trousers, and shirts. We were always on the move to ensure all was done in time for school.

Showers had to be taken in the cold water collected and left standing in the "outdoor bathroom." My mother was not one to be tricked. We all had to be clean to go off to the halls of learning to represent her. We used long grass to brush our teeth and scrubbed our skins with lifebuoy soap. The little house was left in as tidy a condition as possible before we raced off to the one-room school building in Harris—St. George's School.

As soon as school was out in the afternoons, we started back up the road to get home before the four o'clock PWD (Public Works Department) dumper met us on the road. We knew we were late if it ever did, and then we would have to report to Mama. At home, we changed quickly into our house clothes and drank the milk left over from the morning's breakfast or had whatever other food was left over from the morning. We then picked the evening chores to finish before sunset. The animals were brought in, and the yard was swept, with enough time left for a game of marbles, skipping, or whichever game was in season. We tried to squeeze games in before we had dinner and did homework, all ready to read so Mama could hear.

With everyone tired but happy and fed, soon the oil lamp was lit, and we were off to bed to the comforting sounds of chirping crickets, croaking frogs, and barking dogs. They, too, bid the daytime goodbye and settled into their watchful season just outside the door or underneath the wooden floor of the house. Night came quietly and quickly as silence filtered in among the whispers of the night.

Chapter 16

Mother's Heart

Mama was convinced that education was the way out of poverty. We all knew we were expected to work hard at school from the earliest years under her watchful eyes. Fearless and defiant of the odds stacked against her and though burdened with village life where relationships were often strained and tempestuous, she still sent us to school every day.

Sometimes, there was no money to pay for lunches, but our ingenuous mother had made an agreement with a shopkeeper in Harris, where we went to school, to give us bread and some sugar every day. My oldest sister would take the sugar and mix some beverages with the water she got from the lady across the road. We ate quickly and ran back to school to play skipping, marbles, cricket, hopscotch, or whatever was the game of the day. Eventually, as situations improved, she gave us packed lunches, which were usually rice and peas with chicken. Our lunches were left at the home of one of our teachers until lunchtime when we went there to eat.

These were the days of the Seventh Standard Exam and Common Entrance. Every child coming through this system was expected to take the School Leavers' or Standard Seven exams at the end of their nine years of compulsory primary education. They seemed to have been difficult exams because the passes were low.

While there was a Grammar school on the island, it was seen as a place reserved only for the children of well-to-do parents, so only a few students from the "country areas" were allowed to sit the Common Entrance Examination. Teachers (many possibly out of concern, misguided though it was) decided that some parents were too poor to afford to pay for their children to attend were they to pass the exams. The loss suffered and the dreams destroyed as a result are all for another story. Therefore, it was the Seven Standard Exams which most were able to sit. My older siblings all sat the school leaving certificate exam and did well. They were victims of the teachers' misguided judgement.

Successful students whose parents understood how to work through a closed system designed to favour the rich could obtain jobs in the civil service or other prestigious positions available during those trying times.

In the early seventies, my primary school got a new headteacher. Trends were changing, and more and more children from the country villages were getting into the Montserrat Secondary School. It was the gateway to new opportunities and promised freedom from poverty. The time had arrived when more and more schools were judged based on how many secondary school passes they could obtain. Our new headteacher soon cultivated a reputation for producing excellent results at Common Entrance. He set up what he called his scholarship class. We were drilled daily in Verbal Reasoning, Reading Comprehension, Composition, and Mathematics, and from a starting group of possibly twenty pupils, we were soon whittled down to about eleven.

Some days, we saw the others going out to break while we did verbal reasoning, and as our peers passed the time playing rounders, we did compositions. The headmaster was determined that we would be successful. We would be the cream of the crop.

In 1971, our primary school gained more passes than it had ever attained before. It would now be possible for more of us to put on that coveted red skirt and white blouse to get on that bus driven by the respected but sometimes temperamental Mr. Collins. Our headteacher, Mr. Charles Willock, was pleased that St. George's School was well-represented. Another opportunity had indeed proved our school motto, "Knowledge is Power," to be sound and filled with possibilities. He had solidified his reputation as a teacher who got results at the common entrance.

I was one of those who had been successful in the examination. I was initially scared, but my encouraging parents were confident and determined that we would have a better life than they had. Times were tough. The added burden of funding school fees, uniforms, lunches, and bus fare was no easy task. Self-determination and sheer focus spurred my mother. She sweated her way through, spurring our father on to catch the dream she held dear in her bosom.

Trailing in the legacy of success, my younger brother also started attending Montserrat Secondary School two years later.

Chapter 17

Early days at Montserrat Secondary School

That first Monday morning in September 1971, skin well-greased and shining, a bit short for my age, I shouldered my rather large school bag, and with my boy-shoes on my feet, I walked down the hill to the roadside to catch the bus. None of us, as far as I can remember, ever saw the school bus stop at the Village gate. It was a special time for us, the family on Oswald Street.

Little did I realize how proud my other mothers were of my fortune as they all stood by the village stand-pipe to see me off to reach this new milestone in our shared experience. It was a timeless and memorable occasion. One woman, in particular, was there by the stand-pipe, offering her smiling encouragement as I walked solemnly by, afraid to look directly at anyone and hoping none noticed the sweat that seemed to be springing from every pore in my body. She watched until the bus came and left. I knew later that this was a sweet moment amidst the fierce experiences of their collective hopes and desires.

School was a new challenge for me. Having lived with my father's sister in the city before, I knew how it came to be so. But it was such a small city that I got lunch quickly and then hurried back to school to soak up the newness and excitement of such a big school.

As the weeks and months wore on, I was growing more confident. Still, I was a very small and shy person, almost the smallest person in the year group. I learned after a while to defend myself with my sharp tongue, as I had no big brother to defend me and fight my battles if I ever had to muster the courage to engineer any confrontation.

That first year was challenging and, at times, overwhelming; I had no study skills, and I did not want my mother to know how difficult I found some of the lessons. Over the years, I had "skipped classes," so I did not do some year groups. I missed out on some basic skills and knowledge. I failed that first year and had to repeat the first form. But I matured, settled down, picked up the needed skills, and got back on top of my studies. The resilience and doggedness I learned growing up at Oswald Street propelled my onward march.

Getting to school meant I had to rise early, as we still had our chores to complete. Some mornings, I could be seen racing down the hill, barely making it, as some kind soul called out to the bus driver, informing him that I was coming. Even though these occasions were rare, I remember Mr. Collins, who usually refused to wait for latecomers, waiting for me as I ran to catch the bus. I think it was because each morning, I came with a winsome smile and a polite "Good morning" and "Thank you" as I exited the bus.

Chapter 18
More Change

Our parents wanted us to have that spiritual and moral grounding that solidifies and makes effectual academic success. Dada continued buying books from the Adventist colporteurs and sometimes the Jehovah's Witnesses. We had religious books to read, and growing up in the Village, everyone had a knowledge of God and religion. We attended a couple of crusades held by the local Seventh Day Adventists, and soon, my parents were doing Bible studies. One of my older sisters had already joined the church, and unlike my older siblings, I had been offered up there as a baby. I was initially introduced when I used to attend church with my godmother.

Between the late seventies and the early eighties, when my parents started attending and getting baptized into the local Seventh-day Adventist church, all the children, myself and younger, started attending church on Saturdays. The lot of us included my three nieces and a nephew, my eldest sister's children. Eventually, two younger sisters, my two nieces, and I were moved from the local primary school to the Seventh-day Adventist school. A total lifestyle change had begun.

During those years as practicing Seventh-day Adventists, things were not always as pleasant as they could have been. The stranglehold of alcoholism and the human struggle for development in a new way of living sometimes proved more than my father could handle, and he would find himself back at the bottle. What was profoundly notable was that even when he did not go to church on a Sabbath, we knew we still had to go. Mama was always ready. Sometimes, they argued, but not as bitterly as before, and these outbreaks were infrequent.

Our family continued to struggle financially, and my father was unable to find work. Sometimes, there were long periods of little rainfall, meaning crops failed. At other times, when there was a glut on the market, very little came from the sale of produce on market day. Notwithstanding the shortfalls, my father still had to provide for three households.

There was no set minimum wage, and when he hired himself out as a labourer to supplement his meagre income, the additional money went to paying child support for his extended families. We knew securing education was an uphill task, but resilience and hard work kept us going.

Chapter 19

Not Allowed to Work in the Field

It is a strange phenomenon, but our parents and many other villagers were convinced that it was a shame to labour in the fields with a hoe and fork to earn your living. Such work, they felt, was demeaning and smacked of poverty and lack of education. So, from the time I started secondary school, my aunt, my father's sister who lived in town, suggested to my parents that I should not be allowed to work in the field helping out as I had before.

My parents were not in total agreement, so I continued these tasks throughout my years in MSS to assist where I was allowed to. Because of this continued exposure, I learned skills that have served me well so that when I had enough land of my own later, I was able to grow my own food.

My younger siblings and I had a lot of fun picking tomatoes, pigeon peas, and carrots for Mama to sell in the market. After we became Seventh-day Adventists, Mama's market day changed from Saturday to Friday.

I remember some years, sometime during the seventies, when the government managed to secure an export market in Antigua, a neighbouring island, for tomatoes and other goods. After school, we would have to go and carry the tomatoes home to be sorted and packed without them getting bruised to take to the "traffickers" who came down to buy them. We enjoyed racing against each other and having a good laugh together.

One afternoon, as we were engaged in this job, we had to pass by the home of my mother's sister. Being very polite children, we called out respectfully, "Good afternoon, Aunt..." while to her husband, we said pretty cheekily, "Good afternoon..." calling him by his first name. He was certainly not pleased. After we had been rightly reprimanded, being the oldest child present, I decided to demonstrate how to be polite. On our return trip, having ensured our aunt was not within earshot, all six of us (including my nieces and nephew) called out in our politest tones, "Good afternoon, Marse..." We kept this up for the entire afternoon, and as we rounded the corner, we just laughed, having gotten our own back for being told off. Of course, we knew we would be in trouble if we were caught. Our aunt never got wind of it.

There were many days when we would mock and make fun of older people with all the politeness we could muster. We even earned the label of being some of the best-behaved children in the village, except that summer when my little brother and I set fire to the sweet grass, which had almost caught the neighbour's kitchen. We then learned a valuable lesson: "When Karcoo belly full, e cus gad" (When Karcoo's belly is full, he curses God).

We had slept away the rest of that summer afternoon, retiring early after that incident. Never again would Dada have to remind us not to play with fire. It was one of the very few occasions when we learned about the sting of his belt. After no more than three or four strokes, the lesson had been imparted; it was quite enough.

Politeness and good behaviour were fundamental, and it was never acceptable to use any nicknames in the presence of the older folk, who wore these rather strange labels and lived in our thoughts by those very forbidden names. I learned in a shocking way never to say these names aloud, even when you were being polite and meant absolutely no harm.

Family members loved to visit, and I had a great uncle with the most astonishingly booming voice I had ever heard. Long before he arrived, you knew he was on his way. He especially loved my mother, and every time he came, he would spend a long time just sitting in the tiny kitchen, talking and laughing with her. On this occasion, he was on his way up the hill to our little house, and I was on my way down on some errand Mama had sent me on. My bigger brother was also on his way to get water from the standpipe, and he quickly whispered, "You see this man coming up here when you meet him, you must say, 'Good morning, Darda Hoal' (dialect for hole)." Even though he had smirked as he said it, in my innocence, I just did as my big brother had said. Putting on the happiest face and my sweetest smile as he approached, I politely intoned, "Good morning, Darda Hoal."

He suddenly roared at me, and I jumped so far I landed in the grass, shaking with fear. He was calling out to my mother, and I was shaking with fear and shock. Meanwhile, my erstwhile big brother had shot off down the path laughing. Today, he lives in my memory as Uncle Darda.

Chapter 20

Beyond Secondary School

The summer following the GCE exams was a long, lazy oasis of waiting, anxiety, and uncertainty. They had all finished by June, and I waited with expectancy, uncertain of how well I had done. I knew I had worked hard, but that same year, I had been sick with the flu and, for about an entire week, too weak to attend school. I had lost a lot of weight even though I was already lacking in that area.

Exam results came, and as the Lord would have it, I passed all my subjects. My one thought was that I had not let my parents down. There were now some more good results to show for their hard work. There was great rejoicing on Oswald Street.

One morning during that long summer, as I crossed the road on my way back home from a farming task, the school's principal stopped me and advised that he wanted me to continue to sixth form. It was clear that the past five to six years were difficult, especially for Mama, so I made the following decision for her. I knew I could find work, so I refused to go to sixth form. Times were hard; it was time to give back to Mama. That was my great idea. Only time can show to what extent I gave back to her.

I knew she had borrowed money to pay for my O' Level exams. I refused to let her borrow again to pay for books and more exams. My mother cried when I explained why I did not want to go to sixth form; she said it was her decision, not mine. I disagreed. I applied for a job as a primary school teacher. I went to work that summer in the same primary school I had attended as a frightened little 5-year-old (much too short and too small for my age) to help the same teacher who taught me during my introduction to the world of structured learning.

By now, life in the Village had changed and began to evolve as the new generation of younger mothers and young people looked for better jobs and began to embrace more of the trends that were now blowing through the waters of the Caribbean Sea. Many of the characters who had made life hilarious and strange had either died or succumbed to what will now be called by their rightful names: alcoholism, depression, and societal injustices. This mention is merely a nod to the desperate reality of all the losses experienced. The villagers were resilient.

Life in the village was fraught with fun, difficulty, and sometimes harsh and cruel realities. Living on Oswald Street at times mirrored the vicissitudes of village life. It was as if we had to be different yet still be the same. The skills you learned as a young girl would shape the woman you would become.

Our mother taught us the value of hard work and resilience. She taught us to fight, fight the fear and loneliness, and to fight back to keep our independence. She taught us the value of education and ambition. Later on, far from the emptiness of formalized religion, we learned the value of prayer as we listened to her pray early in the morning. How often we would have been saved from trouble if we had given greater heed to that principle.

Our father taught us to be good to people and to help wherever possible. He taught us to rise early, and his love for us allowed us to love our children and put their interests first. This may sound contradictory, but when a father comes home from a day of manual labour (having been on the go long before sunrise), takes down the bag of vegetables off his head, and walks in the pouring rain to get his children from school because of the dangers of flash flooding, it can only be love and duty.

Even though my parents fought and struggled, and as children, we too called each other names and snapped at each other, we all learned that there was a better way. The reality is that heredity and environment will always determine what we become to a great extent.

Chapter 21

Guyana

In September of that pivotal first year, I stood before a class of twenty-odd primary-aged pupils as an untried, eager, fearful young adult. In those days, we were thrust in feet first; one had to learn to stand. Those two years were enlightening, challenging, and happy. The children were a joy to work with, the parents were supportive, and the seasoned staff members were unfailingly kind and always ready to give direction and advice.

After I had taught for two years, the most significant change in my life came when I was sent to the Cyril Potter College of Education in Guyana to study teaching formally. This approach may look a bit like placing one's cart before the horse; however, it enabled us to decide whether we really wanted to be teachers. Life as an adult was undoubtedly here to stay. Those two years at Cyril Potter were some of the best years of my life. It was the first time I had ever lived away from my Village and all those familiar sights that made home warm with certainty and nostalgia.

Under the Burnham government's rule, this vast new country was so different, filled with resources that should have ensured its prominent place on the world stage. Instead, it had a struggling economy, battling food shortages, long bread lines, contraband goods, and petrol shortages. It was a country providing education opportunities for all its many people, but it was also dogged by racism and prejudice.

Life was challenging yet enlightening. I had always heard of Amerindians, but here I was, living in a country where history seemed to come alive right before my eyes. Guyana constantly celebrates its rich cultural heritage and its many peoples. Racial tension is always present, and over the years, there have been clashes that have had devastating effects. Yet Guyana is rich in natural resources, including bauxite, gold, timber, and fertile lands producing rice and sugar cane. Guyana is a country filled with rich treasures, and the Guyanese are resilient and kind.

Montserratians were the only students outside Guyana who trained to be teachers at Cyril Potter College. We consider ourselves fortunate to have been exposed to such a rich experience. I have tremendous respect for the Guyanese people. It is a land of many peoples, various cultures, and languages. I was privileged to meet the descendants of the indentured workers, the descendants of the enslaved people, and the indigenous peoples, all living side by side, interacting and reacting in turbulent and challenging times. Experiencing these various cultures, all blended, was truly vibrant and exciting.

While there, I stayed in Leguan, Corriverton, and Berbice and visited Nickerie in neighbouring Suriname. I loved my years in Guyana. While there were shortages of subsistence items, there really was no shortage of food. People had to learn how to adapt. Rice flour replaced wheat flour, bread was scarce, petrol was in short supply, and sardines were considered contraband. But I was not bothered. I enjoyed the opportunity to put into practice the resilience I learned growing up on Oswald Street. You ate what was in season. If it was breadfruit, you ate breadfruit; when it was sweet potatoes, you ate potatoes.

In the Village, you never let food be a problem, and at home, our mother taught us to be content. Furthermore, I knew I would leave soon. Despite the shortages, I noted it was a land brimming with resources, and its people had learned to use their resources to live contented lives. That indomitable spirit fired their imagination, and they did not just survive; they thrived.

I loved Guyana. I saw first-hand how the developed world can underdeveloped the developing world. It was in Guyana that I saw and experienced racism for the first time. For the first time, I knew being black placed you at a disadvantage, and you were made to feel unequal and different. Yet, I loved this country, the people, their love for culture and education, and the powerful ways in which they learned to cope and, in many cases, excel.

I was no good at socializing with others outside my family and local church circle. I did not trust people easily; whenever I became friends with anyone, it was carefully built and developed over time. I loved and fiercely protected my privacy and the privacy of my family. I never brought home friends from school or visited friends in their homes. The one exception was Yasmin, a sweet soul who had been my friend since secondary school. It is not that my parents discouraged it. We were a large family, and it did not feel right to expose my siblings to outsiders they did not know.

Thus, when I had to leave home, I worried about how I would survive in Guyana. Even though I was going with another teacher, someone I knew well, I knew it would be daunting. I knew I would have to make new friends. Living thousands of miles away from home in a new environment, I had to reach out to others. It could not be business as usual, and I jumped right in.

We had arrived on campus early, and by the time the Guyanese contingent arrived, I was ready to mingle. My roommate Leslin and I became fast friends. I spent many memorable days at her home in Berbice. In her family, I found a mother and father, sisters and brothers in a new and beautiful country; this land was troubled on many fronts, with its charismatic leader determined to defy Western infiltration.

Leslin was my best friend right from the start, and that friendship never changed throughout the two years. As I had successfully formed such a lasting friendship with Leslin, I got the courage to meet others. When teaching practice time came around, I found working with such a great bunch of people quite pleasant. We set about preparing teaching aids, racing through Georgetown to get to schools, and supporting each other in the face of subtle and overt racial prejudice.

Glorene, a college friend, made it possible for me to go on a boat to Nickerie in Suriname. She lived in Corriverton, and these enterprising Guyana nationals learned to trade with their neighbours bringing back supplies for their homes and goods to sell their friends and neighbours. It was a strange adventure. I will never forget the hotel we stayed in, which was shocking and amusing. The rooms were tidy to a fault. I found the street food in Nickerie to be just fantastic.

Education in Guyana was free, and this was the case from the nursery stage to the university level. As a result, students were required to do "National Service." As a foreigner, I was exempt. However, I went with some of my friends just to see what it entailed. Some of it was farm work. I gallantly got myself on the bus with a bunch of less-than-enthusiastic students, prepared to work as hard as the very best of us. Here, I witnessed another side of life for the Guyanese nationals. I saw nationalism at its best and its worst.

Clearly, the workers were imbued with a sense of national pride and were happy to serve their country and, for many of them, their leader. Yet the hardship was visible and heartbreaking, too. I cannot forget the woman I met who told us she married at age fourteen and had eight children. When I met her, she was already forty and was missing a few teeth. But she was so happy and full of laughter despite what I thought was an unfair, harrowing, and unjust experience.

This woman spoke of her joy in her children. She was there because her son would attend university and become a doctor. A mother's love is simple and fervent. Years later, I came to understand what she meant. Life has a way of throwing curve balls. Perhaps how, when, and why we catch it determines the outcome.

I left Cyril Potter College of Education in 1982. I had spent two beautiful years in Guyana, successfully connecting with people from different ethnicities. I had experienced the landscape and the culture and was enriched. The friends I made were invaluable in many ways. They were sisters, friends, counsellors, and just "I have got your back, keep going" supporters.

After an enjoyable, life-changing two-year sojourn, I went back home to write another chapter in the life of a girl from the Village. Did I become wiser and more confident? Who knows? What would be next? Marriage and family?

Chapter 22

Getting Married?

Whoso findeth a wife findeth a good thing and obtaineth favour of the Lord (Proverbs 18:22 KJV)

I do not know whether I was a romantic. At school, I read everything that was within reach. I was an avid reader of romance novels and regularly debated the merits of marriage and children. We would sometimes laugh at boys who became tongue-tied if you smiled at them, always believing that romance lived only in books. Such a notion had no place in the bright light of day.

I think back to the boy I met in secondary school during my final year. He decided that he was going to marry me. I found it hilarious as I never thought much of marriage. But it was his idea of how he would ensure he kept me for himself that I found to be especially comical. He would earn lots of money, so I would not have to work. He was going to build a vast house fenced with high walls and the most updated security system so that no one could take me away from him (and this was the sum of his idea). I was pretty (so he said), and he was ugly (his assessment).

We would be destined for a lifelong marriage of sheer bliss and super control! What more could I want? Such a selfless concept of love and marriage! No wonder such dysfunctionality exists in families and marriages. I was not going to be anyone's idol. Romance existed in books! I was simply being practical.

I always felt I had to fix things for myself. I loved to laugh and to learn. I became highly opinionated, especially if I knew I was right, mostly because I read a lot. I cannot say I had pursued reading with any discrimination. I remember going so far as hiding books in the library while at secondary school so I could find them when I was only allowed to take out two books at a time. I was captivated by romance, mystery, historical fiction, and some West Indian works. I liked reading books on religion. I read the Bible sometimes. I loved the Gospels. I studied the Sabbath School Lessons, not necessarily looking for that deep, spirit-filled experience, but more so because it was more things to know.

Reading was my place of refuge. I felt I needed no one, as after expending that massive effort to make friends in college for the last two years, I was tired. I loved my own company and that of a few people in between my closest friends—all of whom could be counted on one hand and maybe too many fingers. My friends were my family, and at home, I understood later that I was an introvert.

Marrying and marriage was not on my list of priorities. I came home from teacher training filled with new knowledge and a better understanding of child development and how learning takes place. I was excited to get back into the classroom. I knew I had found my niche. I just wanted to teach. I was seeing someone, but it was nothing serious. He was not of our religious faith, and I knew it was not the best thing for me to do much more, so neither of us was ready for any serious commitments. While in Guyana, I started paying more attention to what being a Seventh-Day Adventist meant. But to be a better Christian? Not really.

Chapter 23

The Man of my Dreams?

I met my husband at the SDA church I attended. My heart did not sing with joy but rather smiled with calm interest at the very sound of his voice. Surprise, surprise! Where was the Harlequin, Mills and Boons experience? There was no thought that this was God's answer to my prayer. He was funny, unconventionally honest, good-looking, and ready to please. Even to this day, he has the knack for coming up with some responses that I would blush to say, but coming from him, I just laughed at his audacity.

I did not pray for a prince charming or even a life partner. I was not thinking about marriage. There was more to life than having a boyfriend, much less a husband. The young men in the church had nothing I wanted, or did they? Seeing how other young women faired as they grew up in our village and encountered the obsession with marriage in the Adventist church, where there was just more to expect from life, I felt I had time. Young, confident, assertive, independent, and a trained primary school teacher, I felt marriage, men, and commitments were detrimental to one's health.

My husband was different from anyone I ever dated or became friends with. He was so refreshingly vernal. He was eager to please and anxious to grant my every wish. His interest made me feel flattered. I smiled as I thought that this was just a summer filled with new expectations. Soon, we would move on, working our way into the new persons we were becoming, and laugh about this moment. Nothing more would be likely to happen if I was fair game.

He was fair game. I remember when he said he would marry me; I laughed and told him to come back in ten years. After I laughed, he just repeated it. It was as if what I said did not make sense to him. As I looked contemplatively at him and laughed again, the thought flashed through my mind: *"This kid cannot be serious."* I had no intention of marrying anyone. It was just a passing moment, nothing more.

Five months after we started seriously spending time together, I was pregnant. For the first time in my life, I was scared and worried. Huge questions cascaded one after another, but the biggest worry was this rushing feeling of regret. I felt I had let my mother down; such a painful thought; it was like being hit in the stomach and smashing onto your knees. There was no way back, only onward, but where to? My mind froze with worry. I had to do something, but what?

I spoke to my one friend then, and it was as if I was reporting a story of someone else's life. She listened and asked me the question I had asked myself when I came out of that doctor's office: "What are you going to do?" Maybe this was the time for the modern woman to choose the path of least resistance. Even as the thought touched my mind, I remembered the One whom I would have to stand before. I thought of God, of consequences, of life. Then, I deliberately refused to think. My mind could bring me answers, but it froze as I walked home in a daze.

The night could not speak to me. The mornings brought me misery; morning sickness and annoyance with smells that never bothered me led to Mama knowing even before I finally got enough courage to tell her. By this, we had talked, we looked at the way forward, and our decision was the only one we could honestly take. We decided to get married. Neither of my parents agreed that I should get married. My father was so angry he hardly spoke to me after that. Mama was different. She was not happy; however, I was still her daughter. I was not condemned. But I knew I was not going to be staying at home. This was my responsibility, *our* responsibility, and we had to do it independently.

We spent more time together because I wanted to get away from my father's silence and the pain I suspected my mother felt. Later, I understood that neither Mama nor Dada knew how to express the love they had. All they ever wanted to do was ensure all was well with me. I cannot forget Dada, who said, "I am not sending you anywhere. Come home any time you need to." Their love was always unconditional.

We had a very simple wedding as it was what we could afford. He bought me a simple wedding band. I was happy, he was happy, and we were content. We were finally married. He was twenty-two, and I was twenty-three. We loved each other the best way we knew, and we were confident we could do this. I was convinced that I was smarter than the unfortunate Guyanese woman I had met. I had a career, and I was going to be able to manage it all. Besides, I reasoned, we believed the same things, prayed together sometimes, and studied the Bible together, sometimes. I was spiritually stronger than him, and he was ready to please me. We were set for success.

This marriage was going to work. It was so easy. I would help him become the husband I wanted and be the wife he needed. Indeed, this would not be too difficult; none of that think carefully, depend-on-God routine. He did not drink alcohol or smoke; he was attractive and actively involved in church, even though he was not always keen on studying. It counted, most importantly, that we were equally yoked believers.

He did not enjoy books the way I did. He would listen to the stories I told him with patience and some interest. Still, he never read anything that did not involve practical application and was quite content to go with my opinion on any spiritual matter. He could make me laugh. His one-liners were quick and funny; he just said things as he saw them. I think it was this edgy honesty that I found so interesting, and it later became such a bone of contention. Besides, he worked hard. *This was quite simple.*

We would manage together and smooth over the rough edges. We had enough love and respect for each other, and I was going to shape him into the husband I had conceptualized in those heady days of Harlequin romance and historical fiction.

Besides, what I could not do, God would, so it was already sorted.

I started with the story of the Village, of growing up on Oswald Street, but I had never considered the impact of those early years. Growing up is what we all do; for many of us, what we experience becomes the norm. Intellectually, I knew that the things I experienced were not "normal," at least some of them. They did matter but had just been packed away, stored in my conviction and desire for a perfect life, until I had buried the dysfunction beneath the dormant volcano of deferred expectations.

Education and exposure to different places, people, and attitudes inoculate the individual from the impact of their developmental years. With this in mind, I forged ahead with this mere divergence from my desire to be a twentieth-century independent woman. Percy Sledge sang, "Take time to know her." What about taking the time to get to know me? The past shapes and influences the future in ways that one can never begin to conceptualize. A storm was brewing, and I worked on it with casual nonchalance.

Chapter 24

It Happened

"Marry in a hurry, repent at Leisure?" Is it Biblical?

With confidence and great excitement for the life I had planned for us, we got married on May 1, 1983. I was happy, he was delighted, and we were on a journey. Of course, we had the usual counselling from the pastor:

- Be each other's confidante.

- Do not let the sun go down on your anger.

- Fix disagreements before you go to bed. You only need to shout when the house is on fire.

- Keep him fulfilled and sexually satisfied. Pray together, "The family that prays together stays together."

Then, there was this one that I only understood when the storm hit with unerring accuracy. "There is a sacred circle around the family which no one should enter."

Circle? Sacred? He loved me. I loved him. Our circle was complete—no need to stand at attention. Of course, we understood what the pastor said. I laughed with exuberant expectation as my handsome young boyfriend sweated through these sessions, possibly more concerned about the decision we had made than I was. I did not see why. We both knew what the Bible said. This was an agreement for life, and it was going to last. Nothing else mattered.

Our halcyon days stretched before us in a myriad of lush green eternity. I was his wife, and he was my husband. Two differently quarried diamonds thrust into the unpredictable furnace called marriage.

Those early months before the children came were filled with joy, peace, and contentment. We moved in with his family into what was mostly our apartment. There were two kitchens, so I had my own kitchen, and the living area was basically ours. The bathroom was our only shared space. We had set up a house, and we loved it. I was anxious to get home from school in the afternoons to prepare his dinner and sometimes to experiment with cooking for the two of us. Whatever I cooked was great. He never complained.

We would go for walks, and when he was not mowing lawns to supplement our income, we would walk, laugh, and talk about what I wanted for us or spend hours making love. It was a summer filled with enchantment and excitement.

Gradually, I got bigger, slower, and more irritable. Sometimes, when I ate, the only way to feel comfortable was to stand in the shower and let the water run on my tired stomach. During these untravelled and emotionally charged months, my young husband was patient. We loved each other and laughed a lot. It was a point for amusement when I could not reach my own feet to apply cream or, more truthfully, just wanted him to do it. He would gladly cream my feet and try to ensure he was the perfect husband. We were so happy.

We were always together at church and at home. He was attentive as we basked in the joy of our love for each other and for our baby that was on its way. What could ever disturb this oasis of peace and supportive love, with its promise of a bright future, our own home, a car, and our baby?

Chapter 25

Childhood Experiences Meet Biblical Ideals

Train up a child in the way he should go, and when he is old, he will not depart from it. (Proverbs 22:6)

My young husband had not grown up with either of his parents. In the 1960s, it was common for many young men and women to leave the Caribbean islands for a better life in the mother country, often leaving behind their children with relatives or, in some cases, a neighbour. Left in the care of a benevolent relative, his life was bewildering, carefree, and demanding.

His caregiver was a single parent, and like me, he had several half-siblings from his father. To make things even more complex, she married later in life, but her husband was not the father of any of the household children. My husband grew up with several older second cousins and many other family influences since family ties are often close and, as a rule, families look after each other. Yet it is a fact that Caribbean households can be so complex that it becomes a challenge to decide which lens to use to look at the world around us.

Yet for all that, this godly man, a stepfather husband vested with the duty of care for a ready-made family, stands head and shoulders with the best of men. He became the one constant that enabled this malleable young man, my husband, to understand what it means to be a boy, a man, a husband, and a father. What a challenge it was for so many of our families growing up trying to live respectable lives to recognize that people have to be especially prepared for adulthood. Today, we ask Google? Alexa? AI? No, it has to be demonstrated and taught.

My husband would recall with profound respect the patience and kindness of his "old man." This man of God was a unique and astute father to each of the children in this extraordinary household. He would smile fondly, remembering how this alternate father addressed him as "Old Fellow." His stepfather's work ethic and moral values gave him some simple practicalities for his approach to marriage and family life.

Besides, there were the practical skills he learned from his adult second cousins. Yet the gaps created were so deeply ingrained, and at times, the tracks of habit proved so deep that it was often difficult to build over or adjust to a new reality.

Life in some of our households remains enigmatic and problematic. Which piper plays the lead tune? Regarding his biological father, he readily recognized that he had not done much for him. Even though he passionately believes that his father did love him, he would speak with regret and profound sadness of times when he never returned with the money he had promised to bring to provide for his upkeep. It was this that made him decide that if he ever made a woman pregnant, they would have to marry so he could have all his children under one roof. Is this strange? Is the cart once again before the horse? We built it that way in our simple belief that we had enough to live on and more besides.

We were prepared to make this a success. We thought little of the challenges ahead; the truth is, we knew nothing. Being young and confident, for us, the glass was half-full. When our sons arrived in September of that year, we had to learn fast and adapt quickly to work together. We were in the midst of a perfect storm but still did not know it. All around us were people who cushioned and helped us; it was a wonderland for the young couple with the twins.

We knew we loved each other and our children. Every Sabbath, we were in church. Since we were surrounded by all that should make for a perfect family, we just needed to keep swimming upstream, and the incoming tide would never disturb the anchor we had so bravely buried in the sea of marriage. We would learn together how to be husband and wife, parents and individuals, with our ideals, aims, and personalities.

Chapter 26

Heredity or Environment?

Nature or nurture: only time can tell the extent to which these two ideas define one's life. Despite the best efforts made in many of our nuclear and extended households by mothers, the absence of a father figure will always have a lasting impact. Lack of contact with a solid male character will remain debilitating for equipping boys to become men. We have come to know and expect that a man ought to love his wife, provide for his children, and, in spiritual contexts, be the priest, making decisions towards making life better day by day.

In the best way, he knew how my young husband agreed with me on making our life together a success. We knew what our family needed. While growing up on Oswald Street, I had learned early on how to manage the house chores, including changing diapers, and at times had to take charge of the behaviour of my younger siblings and my nieces and nephew. I now add the task of keeping hold of my career. I was all at once *Eve*, I was *Martha*, and I aspired to be *Abigail*. However, I became overly preoccupied with looking after our temporary home. It was my world, and I accepted it with the confidence of a woman of strength. Each night, I went to bed tired but happy that we were together and could raise our boys to be men of worth.

My enterprising and concerned husband worked two jobs so we could eventually earn enough to have our own home. Now, we could lock our doors and never have to worry about the presence of others within a shared space. In our previous abode, family members were often present, though supportive, but the present privacy brought relief despite how supportive they had been, and my husband's family was very supportive. Yet we worked so we could move.

Neither of us had any real time that belonged to us. It was always a juggle between our daily nine-to-four, his extra job, and looking after the children. We were constantly on the go, hardly ever thinking how much more we needed to be there for each other. I wanted our marriage to work, yet as I looked back, I did not know what a working marriage looked like. Both of us were certain the answer lay in our shared ideals and dedication to our children's happiness. We thought it would just happen as we did the right things and ticked all the boxes.

Hubby took for granted that teaching, disciplining, and training was what the mother did. He often reassured me, "I love you." No matter how pressing things were, he made it a rule to repeat and demonstrate those three powerful words as best he could. I heard the words but did not always take the time to absorb them or trust them. Looking back at all those turbulent years on Oswald Street, I never heard either of my parents use those words to each other. Mama would tell us ever so often we were her "pride and joy." That says, "I love you." My father told me years later, "I loved your mother from the start; she just never looked my way in those early years." Therefore, I was not going to be soppy.

My husband worked hard. I saw it, accepted it, and even appreciated it, but I also wanted him to be everything else and more understanding of everything. How was he to learn the skills he needed to be a man, father, and husband, especially when they all snowballed into each other with little warning? But still, I felt we were doing great meeting those undefined standards that sit at the centre of any intimate relationship.

Basking in the splendor of our own sunshine, laughing together, walking together, keeping the house as one, resplendent in support of both sides of our extended and church families, all was well. There is still a sacred circle that none should enter. Even when the rumblings began, and the earth under my feet shook, I laughed when we argued, often for something and nothing.

Chapter 27

Who Needs a Counsellor?

We were in church every Sabbath, and I loved Sabbath school. The energy shared, and the knowledge imparted could be gotten from nowhere else. It was a safe place where families could learn, share, and grow. The twins were still a novelty, and everyone wanted to help. Despite the known goodwill and kindness of the church family, I was a picky mother. I would help with other children when I sensed the cry for help from mothers, especially the young ones, but as a rule, I never had that desire to be rapturous and overly hands-on with other people's babies, and I certainly did not want too many others to be like that with our children. I was constantly watching to see where they were.

At home, I was the same. This constant need to be in control and to have clear routines was ever present with me. My husband was always willing to be relaxed and open and was an unfailing peacemaker. He was not too bothered, quite unaware even, and could see nothing wrong if the children were with people outside our family circle. At times, I did not see how tired he was or, at times, almost clueless. Later, I understood much better that it was not his fault. He was not being deliberate and lacking in understanding and empathy; he simply did not know. There, in our perfect world, a silent squall completely unnoticeable was settling in. With so much time dedicated to being parents and my obsession with being all in all for our young family, we grew apart even as we worked together.

It is not that we lack resources that would have enabled us to turn the tide and dispel the storm; we simply took no time to see where we were headed. There was no shortage of time-tested material to help make our home a little heaven here on earth, no shortage of practical guidance. But we paddled into the deep without a proper decision as to who should be the captain, and as the seas got rougher, we were floundering. The deep truth that we missed was that despite where we had come from when we come to God, He equips us with all the resources to supply any lack. After all, He is our Father. Was it not true? Has he not promised to supply every need "according to His riches in glory by Christ Jesus?" (Philippians 4:19, KJV).

In *The Adventist Home*, my favourite author, Ellen White, reminds men they are the "house band" while she tells the mother she is the "queen" of her household. That is just about right. But who was thinking of such lofty ideals? Not me. Not us. We said the right things and appeared in the right places.

It wasn't easy being parents and learning to be husband and wife at the same time. I can admit that now, but in those early eighties, we never really thought about it. We both worked and shared as much responsibility as possible since I wanted everything to be perfect, but life was demanding. It took some adjusting, and in the process, as diamonds in the rough, we cut and hurt each other.

There were days when we shone at home, but little strange silences filled the rooms except for the laughter or crying of our children. But we were the golden couple; we had *twins*, and people liked to talk about and admire the twins. But no one saw the strain or heard the exchange of sharp words. The bright smiles would come out every time we went into the public.

Most times, I felt I was the one being wronged, and as such, impatience was never far from the surface. I was always convinced that I was the proverbial good wife: always up early, getting the children washed and ready to go, having dinner prepared in good time and tasty, and providing enough intimacy to ensure we were both sexually fulfilled. That had to be all that was expected. Yes, I really tried to be a good wife.

But maybe there was another truth about individuality, compromise, and independence that I was unwilling to learn or even consider necessary—the truth about biblical submission. The truth is, for me, submission was conditional. I understood only after I had failed again and again that submission in marriage can be dependent on individual perceptions or socialized behaviours. I will be bold to speak for my husband.

We loved each other unconditionally, so we thought we had no need for counselling. However, we both had different ideas of love and what it looked like, so we sometimes disagreed. We also had our burdens and insecurities, things we did not understand or, at times, did not wish to face.

Since the ideal for a happy marriage is embedded in the twin concepts of submission and love, like a beautiful diamond on a pillow, it is no wonder we struggled and lost our way so many times. Neither of us had taken the time to polish and protect these two concepts.

Some modern psychologists may say we needed counselling. Maybe we did, perhaps we do. Those subtle truths were given in those age-old sayings of the Villagers: "teet' and tongue will bite."; "long grass carry news"; "no hang you dirty linen a road" possibly fuelled the reticence to seek help.

Theoretically, I believed that it was only the counsel of God we would ever need. It is such a beautiful theory; God's counsel makes all the difference. It is He whose truth is sharpest and yet the most restorative. That this truth was there somewhere in my subconscious was great, but so often in my struggles, it was the hardest to institute. I knew Him theoretically, but the practicality was so very different altogether. Like the women who strove against all odds in the dark days of sharecropping, I had to apply my solution. Yet how often I had said to others in crisis, "Tell it to God; He knows."

His counsel is accessible to all who hear His voice. Of course, I know that I did not read the Bible, study the Sabbath school lesson, and have worship (when I could). I smile as I think about these things: such a practical Christian (all in the head). Talk is so cheap, and obedience so difficult. I could repeat these deep convictions glibly. Here it comes: "Sometimes, He tells us to seek help from his servants. Other times, He simply binds up our wounds and pours oil on them: the oil of His healing balm of forgiveness, restoration, and love." Am I in need of a counsellor? Oh dear, no. I have this one.

Chapter 28

Days of Adjusting

In the months leading up to the birth of the boys, I would argue much with my husband. I felt my superior knowledge of everything gave me the right to direct our lives. Our arguments were always quickly fixed as I had to sleep curled into his back, and only when I slept like this did the babies keep still in the womb. We were in love, and I thought nothing of my impatience and quick temper.

Things got into a workable pattern. I was at home for two months. I woke up early in the morning and my husband helped me with the washing and bathing. In fact, even though he worked full time and did lawns after work, he still helped around the house as much as possible. Some nights, he had to be up to help as the boys would wake up together. Sometimes, he fell asleep with one or both in his arms. Looking back, I should have known he was tired. I did not want to know. I just got mad at him and snapped at him.

By the time I had to go back to work (I was a primary school teacher), it was tough. Early in the morning, while the boys slept, he would wash nappies and baby clothes and then go to cut lawns. I would cook and try to get the boys ready, as he had to take one to my mother while the other was cared for by his aunt. It seems we were always on the go as we juggled work and caring for our twins.

Despite all the help we got from the extended family, we set aside very little time for ourselves, and whenever we did, we used these breaks to prepare for the next dose of ceaseless activity. The strain on both of us began to show; arguments were more frequent and painful. I would sleep on the edge of the bed so he could not touch me. When we did not argue, I would lie with my head on his shoulder, his arms around me, or curled up in his back, comforted by the present peace and respite.

Sometimes, on Sabbaths, my sisters and mother would take the boys home so I could go home to sleep. We attempted to take these little oases to enjoy each other's company. I loved to read, and I would insist he read with me or study the Bible with me. He would often fall asleep, but I did not accept that he was tired and not as interested as I was in reading.

Even though I let him sleep, anger and annoyance burned within me. I would go quiet and refuse to speak to him. Little things would become big things, and almost everything seemed to be a problem. Realising how much strain we were under; we made a greater effort to be more accepting of each other as we tried to stay upbeat.

For a while, when things were going well, we agreed we could not manage any more children, and we decided that I would use "the pill." I had been warned that it is not the best method of contraception as it leads to reduced interest in intercourse, but since it was so easy to remember to do, I went with it. Those days were when one trusted the doctors implicitly and hardly expected to be given poor advice.

In a few short years, it began to take its predicted side effect, along with the fact that, at times, I was just too tired. I started to find excuses for not making love, and since I did not want to take responsibility for this outcome, I let the contraceptives take the blame. Besides, I was beginning to spend more time in prayer and easily convinced myself that God would not allow us to get pregnant as long as we prayed.

My husband was becoming frustrated with what he saw as my excuses, and as man-like as he could, he did everything he could so I would have time for him. I laugh, but it is true; he really put in extra time. I must admit that God answered our prayers, though I did not think so at first. I stopped taking the pill, and three years later, I was pregnant again. We had prayed that God would take care of the contraception—now there was another baby to care for.

The arguments started again. I was worried it might be another twin, but of course, I never shared my deep concern. I could not see how we would manage, so I blamed him. Again, he tried to be patient, explaining that we would just get extra work, and returned to my own words: Wasn't I not the one who kept saying God would provide? I listened, but fear made me hear all the difficulties we could expect.

Let me hasten to say our arguments were never about the children. It was always about what was the best way forward. I hardly ever let him make the final decision. Despite the fears I carried as the months passed, I became content. We became content and worked together to keep the harmony that is so foundational to a happy home. As soon as the baby came, we had months of peace. It was like an oasis in the troubled sea of our three years of marriage. We had a daughter this time, my "Lady." This was a much easier birth, and our little girl enthralled us. She was a Lady from the day she arrived. Her dad was well-pleased; she was his little princess. Her brothers called her "madam" and were pleased to show off their little sister. They were her most ardent protectors, always ready to sit with her, to protect her, and later to defend her from any imagined threat. We were fine. Money was tight, but we were getting by. We were so happy.

My husband liked getting me gifts for my birthday, Christmas, and anniversary. I enjoyed buying him things, too. Somehow, while I always seemed to get him something he loved, he was not always as adept at getting what I liked. I was, at times, rude about his gifts and unappreciative of the effort he was making. Years later, with maturity and spiritual eyesight, I realized he was simply easier to please than I was. He would say he had grown accustomed to hand-me-downs all his life, so getting something new made him feel so grateful.

I would get mad when he did not get it right, so he started giving me money to get what I wanted. As I said before, we did not have much money, so I often spent the gift money on getting things for the children or groceries we needed, which would upset him. I would try to make him believe it was good practical sense, but he disagreed. I snapped at him. I pushed. He pulled back. We did not see where we were headed.

We both enjoyed serving in church, and he was the Pathfinder Club Director. That is a club within the Adventist church centered around ministry and recreational activity for the youth. When he took the Pathfinders camping, I once went with him as the camp cook. It was fun for all because we were the perfect family. Despite all the strain, we were holding things together. We would go for long walks on Sabbath afternoons with the children.

To all appearances, all was well. We were the golden family. It was fun for all because we were the perfect family. The first seven years were normal despite our arguments, which, as he pointed out, often remained unresolved if I did not get the desired results.

Our lives revolved around the children. It was work, church, taking care of the children, and then more work. Besides going to church on Sabbath, we attended meetings on Sunday and Wednesday evenings. So, one would ask, why the angst?

We took so little time to be a couple. We were growing up and apart, utterly unaware of the hurt we were causing each other. Like the women in the Village, I was working parallel to him.

The independence I had developed was sometimes counter-productive to the oneness that makes a successful marriage.

Chapter 29

Moving Back to Oswald Street

We lived with my husband's aunt for a time as we did not have our own home. It was okay, at least for the time. The living area was perfect for when the twins started moving around. We argued, but sometimes it was not too awful, or so I thought.

It was not a typical shouting-slanging match; only it subtly mined away trust, support, kindness, and patience. "I am more intelligent than you are." "You are headstrong." "I earn a bigger salary." "You cannot tell me what to do." "Why are you so silly?" "Why are you so quick to get angry?"

The silences were the easiest and most detrimental to our stability. In the Village, one learned to mask the pain. Some drank, some screamed, some became physically abusive. I hated noise. Ironic, isn't it? I kept quiet after the explosions as I remembered the hurt, fear, and anxiety. I again asked myself how these women who nurtured the upcoming generation while remaining purposeful did it. Did they explode in their hearts, broken with pain, yet made the determination to live on?

I would refuse to speak to him for days as self-preservation forged above the desire to reconcile. He was not like that. At times, I thought it was like throwing water on the back of the proverbial duck. Who or what had forged this spirit of "if you won't leave it, I will talk it out of you?" Again, I look back at the hilarity and glee of the Village, the storms setting up in Farrell's Mountain, and the mist consuming Oswald Street. These were the furnaces in which I was forged. *This, too, shall pass.*

In the meantime, he was a talker, so he would try to make up quickly, and I would ignore him or respond only in monosyllables. He often pointed out that remaining silent would not fix anything. I would tell him he did not listen. It took me years to understand that what I thought was simple, straightforward, and obvious was, in fact, deeply complicated and that, at times, I was the one who did not listen. I did not listen to his plea for understanding, his plea to tell him things in simple ways. Words often flooded out in rivers of annoyance. I did not hear his cry for help.

He, too, did not listen, apparently impervious to my plea for understanding. I would feed him a spate of information facts mixed with my emotional understanding of the situation, but he did not get it, so I insisted he was not listening.

We had been living with his family for about two years, and my independent spirit drove me to push to have our own home. We acquired land in the Village not far from where my parents lived. We joined a government scheme that provided a grant for houses. Since I had grown up there, we were able to purchase the land at a relatively affordable price. We did not have the finances to get it done, and my husband took on much of the preparation and labour. He worked hard to get it done. We got it completed to a standard where it was habitable. We intended to finish it before we moved in, but that did not happen.

One Sunday, we had a terrible argument. I do not know how or why it started. I packed my things, called a family friend to come and get us, and left with the children. I told my father he tried to hit me. This was *my* version of the truth. My father threatened to shoot him. I refused to return to the house we lived in prior, so we now had to move into our unfinished home. He did what he could, so we had a place to live.

Once again, we were okay. It was our own home. We had a new start. We loved each other, laughed, and spent more time with the children. On some Sabbath afternoons, we took the children for long walks. On Sabbath evenings, we had worship together, but on some weekdays, when he left to cut lawns in the early mornings, I would have worship with the children before they left for school. By the time he returned to get ready for work, breakfast would be prepared as he ate quickly and hurried out to take the children to school.

On Saturday evenings, we went into the city center and ate hot dogs and ice cream as we sat on the beachfront. During the week, the twins would get up early in the morning and go with their young cousins to look after the cattle and sheep. I did the chores while their little sister listened to her Bible stories on the radio cassette player—the ancient equivalent of today's iPods.

The mornings were filled with getting the children off to school, washing, cleaning, and getting to our separate jobs on time. Yes, things were looking up, and a gentle warmth settled in our home in the heart of Oswald Street.

Chapter 30

Shifting Times

The Family Circle is a sacred circle around every family which should be preserved. No other one has any right in that circle; the husband and wife should be all to each other. (Ellen White, The Adventist Home, p 177:2)

One of the things I was sure of was that no matter what we faced, our marriage would remain. As time passed, there seemed to be a strange element putting strain on our relationship. It had to do with friends who seemed to be demanding more of his presence and time. When we disagreed about this, I sometimes got mad enough to threaten him with divorce. I wasn't really serious. It was a card I played to get what I wanted. I never thought that we would ever separate.

I remember even saying to him that should I die; I would like him to marry this or that person because I knew my children would be fine with her. He told me I was crazy; we would always be together. He added that if I died, he would not marry anyone else because his children were more important than any other woman could ever be, and so he would have to learn to care for the children by himself. That sounds like an odd conversation, especially when you are both young and the world is before you.

Infidelity was something that happened to *other* people. In our idyllic little world, nothing could take away our commitment to each other, our children, and our family. We would *never* be unfaithful.

Those early days were good, in spite of the occasional disagreements and my silence. By now, he had changed jobs. He had bought us a car and insisted that I learn to drive. This new job would cement what we wanted to build: a home for our expanding family. With this job change came also a change in his circle of friends and associates. It was a challenging time, with three young children and a demanding profession.

I know that, at times, I was not my best at school. I was tired physically, mentally, emotionally, and, at times, spiritually. My extended family was a harbour, my support network. My sisters helped; my mother helped. The cycle of life was school, home, shopping, and church.

Things were changing, but I was too busy caring for the children and working. I did not see it or possibly refused to acknowledge it, even when I knew we talked less. I just did what I knew a wife and mother must do to hold things together: listen to those soulful country and western ballads, sometimes pausing to look at the gently rolling hills in front of our home and the shimmering blue of the Caribbean Sea with its promise of calm, hope, and laughter.

In my way, I wanted my husband to enjoy some of his forfeited youth, so I was happy for him to engage in one of his best-loved strengths, his ability to sing. He had joined several singing groups, and I loved going to concerts where he performed. He sang beautifully. He was attractive and friendly. I thought nothing of his increasing popularity with the sisters. I loved only him. He could love only me.

He seemed to be increasingly acquiring an interesting array of friends, all of the opposite sex. Surely, these were none other than fair weather clouds. Often, he shared tales of these waifs, strays, and damsels in distress who confided in him. As I listened, I became cautious and troubled. I didn't want to come across as jealous or controlling, so I alerted him that this wasn't right. It was not the right thing to do. Of course, we disagreed.

Blinded by self-importance and naivety, he was unable to see. *What could be so wrong?*

People give all kinds of reasons why men or women cheat. Some seem plausible, and some people go as far as to say in some cases, it is justifiable. But I want to state from the outset there is no justifiable reason for any partner in a marriage to cheat. I am convinced of that now more than I have ever been. We cheat because we are selfish. Plain and simple. You see, "No temptation has overtaken you except what is common to mankind. And God is faithful; he will not let you be tempted beyond what you can bear. But when you are tempted, he will also provide a way out so that you can endure it." (1Corinthians 10:13 NIV). When our minds are surrendered to God, He defends us, and in a marriage, we must learn to live for each other and not simply for ourselves.

We are told many things during counselling in preparation for marriage. One truth that made me realize how sacred a marriage must be is a quote from the book *The Adventist Home*. The author writes, "There is a sacred circle around the family which no one should enter." The Bible tells us a man should "cleave to his wife." Often, church members are busybodies; they tear down where they should build up. While sin lies at the door of those involved in relationships between husbands and wives, husbands and wives must always take their concerns to God and no one else.

Marriage counselling has its place. I am talking about the habit we develop of exposing the faults and shortcomings of our partners to a third party. My favourite author writes in the book Adventist Home, "The heart of the wife should be the grave for her husband's faults, and the heart of the husband should be the grave for the wife's faults."

We both learned the hard way what that meant.

By now, we had three children and were living in our own home. An opportunity came for me to study and work in Special Education. It was a two-year course in Jamaica. We talked about it, and he agreed I could go. Everything was being worked out. The twins were around seven, and our daughter was about four. In reality, he did not want me to go. He worried about how he would manage on his own. He did the only thing he felt he could do.

He went and got a lady he knew I would listen to and explained what he felt. She advised me not to go. I gave up the opportunity, but I was so mad at him. I thought he was just being silly and immature. Years later, I was happy he had stopped me from going.

He had a new set of friends. His life was filled with work, cutting lawns, and going to rehearse and perform with his singing groups. I just kept looking after the kids because, at times, I felt he needed the company of other men. He was so young when we got married, and we had our children so soon. We were growing apart.

I liked intellectual stimulation. I was not getting it. I had no time for friends. I had my children. We were constantly arguing. I felt the intimacy in our marriage was fine. He disagreed. I became annoyed with him. I felt he expected too much. I started thinking about a career change and went off to law classes. He encouraged me and was quite pleased. More and more, I felt he was becoming too friendly with other women, and he sometimes stayed out late. I would sit and talk with a friend who encouraged me to be more open with my husband and show him more love.

I was enjoying the evening classes, finding the intellectual stimulation I needed. This was 1991. However, I was now pregnant for a third time and was often too sick to manage the extra classes. Besides, the worries I had with the increasing presence of female friends hovered like dark shadows over the peace of our marriage. A new job with a better salary came his way, and as ever, we took it without understanding that it is

God who gives and trusting Him was the only sure way forward.

At his new place of work, I came to know quite a few of the men. I learned how readily one can be influenced by the values and attitudes of those with whom we associate. I think growing up in the Village, at times, made the unacceptable become acceptable.

I paid little attention to how this new environment could affect our relationship; after all, we were SDA Christians, and I was confident my husband would be fine. Despite the darkening shadows, we both assumed it would be well. Most of the time, I would be so caught up with my daily existence that important events would be buried in the reservoir of my busyness.

My husband has a great memory, and often, when I could not remember the date for some important event or information, I just had to call him; he would give me the place, the time, and even a record of who had been present. In this regard, he was my retrieval bank. He was also quite romantic. At times, the unexpected gestures would bring laughter that created star-filled moments, dispelling the gloominess of raising children and holding down demanding jobs.

One such delightful occasion occurred when I worked at Bethel Primary School. I had forgotten about our anniversary, and a florist arrived at the school with the most amazing bouquet of white roses. To this day, whenever I think of what is great about my husband, that spills into my mind, and I smile with hope and peace. Surely, with such devotion, infidelity was unimaginable.

Chapter 31

The Unthinkable

I knew things were going wrong when he started coming home late on Fridays. One, two, three...a pattern was forming. I confronted him about it. He said I was treating him like a child. Well, maybe I was. I told myself that I did not need to worry again. He needed a social outlet. But nothing much changed. Even though I was angry, I forced myself to be patient and resorted to prayer. Then, I completely lost it one weekend, and an avalanche followed that incident.

That Friday, he was later than usual, and to add to that, I could smell alcohol on his breath. I was having none of this. I was tired from a long week at school and had to prepare the house for Sabbath. I was mad. I just acted out whatever came to my head. I made a huge scene. I threw away his dinner and turned up the bed when he tried to get in it. I did not think about the children and how they were affected. They were watching their nature program on television.

All I could think of was how often I had told him of my dislike for alcohol drinking and the difficulties we had experienced as children because of it. He never did anything except to ask me to stop. I was not listening. Anger, frustration, and tiredness all erupted in a furious flow. This was too much.

The storm smouldered on as he went and complained to my parents. I was reprimanded in no uncertain terms for throwing away his food. I was out of order. For days, silence reigned. I knew he was sorry but did not want to hear anything. I could not see the point of being sorry for doing something inconsiderate and thoughtless. When I cooled off enough, I made that perfunctory nod to the God I claimed to believe in. Did I not say we were Christians? Where, then, is your God?

As ever, I had this one. As my father explained why my actions were extreme and unnecessary, I stood defiantly in front of him, determined in my mind that I was not the one who had caused the problem. While I listened to my father, I raged in indignant silence that it was not his business to tell me what to do. He had no right. The man knew I hated anything to do with alcohol. This was not going to happen again. Not ever. It never did.

Yet things only kept going downhill. It was soon after this incident that I realised I was pregnant a third time. At first, I just wept and wept. How were we to manage? I had just started going to law class. Now, I know that God never makes a mistake. Being pregnant then was right for me; I did not see it to be so at the time.

I had to drop out of law class because I was pregnant. I was angry, and continually, I blamed him for the pregnancy. He tried to reason. I shut him out, and the only time I was not mad at him was when I was at work or when it was just the children and me at home. I tried to keep things as normal as possible for them. We went to church; my daughter was learning to play the piano, and they all went to Pathfinders. They went camping and were engaged in club activities, providing a safe environment to build lasting and trustworthy friendships.

Their father was spending more time with "friends." The interesting thing was he never stopped helping at home. But by this time, he was openly involved with someone else. Later I discovered it was more than one person. As always, he unswervingly insisted they were just friends.

By this time, the twins were ten, our daughter was seven, and the baby was one year old. I tried to make him stop his affairs.

I reasoned with him on biblical grounds and talked about the impact on the children and how it made me feel but to no avail. When he bothered to respond, he was convinced that he was not hurting his children, and besides, there was no point in trying to keep a marriage going for the sake of children.

In all this, I prayed and cried to God, but it was always with the idea to get rid of the other woman. It was *her* fault, and it was *his* fault, and it was not mine. I was going to brave it out. I made demands, I cried, I kept silent. Things only became worse.

Chapter 32

My Solution

I prayed sometimes, all the while living for my children. I felt I had to protect them, not knowing then that I was teaching them values that ran counter to becoming strong adults. My husband would tell me he was not a child whenever I asked where he was going. Before all this came to the fore, there were complaints about our sex life. It is possible he was right, but I just told him he was unreasonable.

It was a never-ending cycle of complaints, reasoning, and silence. The more the complaints came, the more the atmosphere spoke in silence as I would shut down, refusing to communicate with him. I spent more time on the phone with my girlfriend than speaking to him. He complained that he did not know what to talk to me about because we continuously argued, and I was convinced he was not listening.

He would go to his social groups while I stayed home with the children. I hardly had any friends. Caring for the children took up all my time. I was obsessed with them and did not want to leave them with anyone because they were my responsibility.

I knew things were bad, but I could not seem to find a way out of the maze we were in. I could not tell him how I truly felt; I was unsure he wanted to know. What about church? We kept going to church, and we still sat together. Ours is a small community, so soon, other people knew he was having an affair. It was the usual response (from a society that still thought it was okay for a man to cheat but a disgrace for a woman to do the same thing) that many people thought nothing of it.

I spoke to a friend of mine about how I felt. I was angry with the other woman. I hated her. I spent hours complaining and bewailing about the wickedness of these "other women." My friend told me one night, "She is not the problem. You cannot fight with her or even with your husband." He told me to fight with God. Let God make him into the husband you want him to be.

Ridiculous! Fight with God? Let God fix him. I just never understood how right he was until years later. Things became terrible; we fought constantly, and he took every opportunity to leave the house. One night, as we argued long after the children had gone to bed, I said, "At times, I feel like poisoning you." To this day, I do not know why I had said something so awful. Now I know that a mind not under the control of God is a mind under the power of the enemy of all good.

I remember the book "Heart of Darkness," in which the main character could not explain how he could have gotten involved in trading slaves. I think years later of the Bible verse that says, "The heart is desperately wicked, who can know it?" Words are deadly. Of course, I did not mean that, but he believed it, and maybe rightly so. He refused to eat what I cooked. He got into the habit of getting the children to taste the food before he ate it. Again, in a fit of outrage that he believed I would harm him, one afternoon, I picked up the plate and tossed it through the door when he tried to have one of the children taste his food before he ate it. Wrong move. That convinced him. Or did he want to be convinced?

Chapter 33

No End in Sight

It was not long before the atmosphere became even more volatile. The pain was buried in the pride of sarcasm and deep silences. Other women had set up their advice agencies. "You are not wrong." "She is trying to control you." The sisters felt qualified to offer advice and make judgements.

I think what made me the angriest was when I realized that these women were also members of the church. I convinced myself it would not have been so heartbreaking if they had not heard the same sermons I heard. It would be better if they did not know they should not be involved with married men, whether in church or out. I levelled all my anger and frustration at them.

It was not just the actual other women only; it was all their friends who seemed to have made it their business to become close friends with him as well. One of these "friends" got her little sister to call my home and told her, "If his wife answers, just hang up." I was constantly on edge. The arguments just pushed him further and further away. I cried, I threatened, I kept silent.

Eventually, we separated. He moved out, and I was left alone with four children. By this time, the twins were eleven, my daughter was eight, and my younger son was just two. I remember the morning after he left, I could not face going to work. There was one friend I was close to at that time. She was the one person who came to my wedding who was not of my immediate family. We had been friends throughout my years at secondary school. We both became teachers and attended teachers' training college the same year. We would meet up in town sometimes at the month's end. We even went away on holiday together at one time. She has always been my friend.

I called her, too broken to go to my parents who lived next door. She brought a friend with her, a godly woman who believed in the power of prayer. She prayed. I cried. I blamed my husband. I blamed the other woman. It was not my fault. I was the victim, and he was the villain.

I was comforted, somewhat. I had to tell my mother he was gone. I love my mother. She never made me feel it was my fault. She just made it clear that she was there. I knew my family would be the support I needed. I had never told them how it had been. It was my problem. I was the one who had married him; it was my responsibility. I told her it was not her problem.

I did not involve my parents because people already believed they were too involved in my affairs; at least, that was how my husband presented it. The fact was that nothing was further from the truth. My mother gave us financial help. She helped me pay the children's school fees. She knew how tired I was sometimes, so she would cook so I did not have to. My sisters helped me look after the children. I love my family.

I had to face the world. I went to work and sent the children to school. At night, I cried. I continued as the days turned into months, and the months became years. I laughed and worked. Growing up on Oswald Street had taught me resilience. The women on Oswald Street did what they had to do. I was bent almost out of shape, but I held the responsibility of caring for my children. We had worship, and I helped with homework, but most of the time, my sister would get their homework done.

At nighttime, I cried. In the morning, I went to work. Their dad took them to school every day. He also came and mowed the lawn and fixed anything that needed fixing in the house.

Chapter 34

A Counsellor?

During all the turmoil, pain, fighting, and blaming, I had a friend. I am going to call him Sammy. He is simply a star. This young man just talked me through my anger at times. We used to discuss the Bible for hours. My husband always said he did not need to worry about Sammy and me.

Sammy was a Christian; he truly loved and served God. His advice was invaluable, as he constantly reminded me that blame would make no difference. He always insisted that I look for the way forward. He was already a counsellor long before he became certified as a marriage counsellor.

It was Sammy who made me realize two things. He was confident that one spouse could fix a marriage with God's help and that women too often channeled their anger in the wrong direction. He pointed out that it was not the other woman who was the problem but the man. He insisted there was no point in finding fault with the other woman since it would always be another one if it were not this one. He pointed out that we wasted energy fighting each other while the guilty party got away with his perfidy.

I fought my way through those years. I was always busy working, looking after the children, and going to church. I was angry sometimes. I would flip at the slightest error the children made. I was not a cruel or violent mother. I did not smack them unnecessarily. I was very strict with them, and they learned the things to avoid doing as they grew older. They were my sole focus, reason to keep going, and inspiration to learn to be calm and strong.

They all went to Pathfinders. I sent the three older ones to our denominational school. They sometimes spent time with their father. Not that I wanted them to; however, when the reasonable person in me asserted herself, I knew it was the right thing to do.

During this pain-filled time, I found support and solace with another girlfriend. She was my sounding board for everything. She was a Christian, though not a Seventh-day Adventist. She was just chock full of kindness. Between her and Sammy and looking after my children, I managed to keep afloat. I knew about God. I spoke to Him. I held morning worship with my children.

The sad reality was that I did not know God. The idea of Him was very present, but some nights, I had worn myself out enough physically and mentally that I just went to sleep, awakening the next day to do the same things. The most peace I had was when I thought of my children and how I had to keep going for them. God was always there. I just never trusted Him to lead in the way He would have had I allowed Him to.

In the early days of our separation, a few people from our church came by, but I did not speak much with them. I listened to the elders. One down-to-earth, kind woman from the Village who lived above us would often call out, and she prayed for us. One very dear old sage told me, "He is your husband. Keep yourself only for him." Strange advice? No, it was kind and definitely God-inspired.

Again, I am reminded that when the villagers got married, they were married for life. It was not always the right choice. It was the one they believed in, and again and again, it was the concept they espoused. They made it plain they were there to help. I was and still am a very private person. Smilingly, I accepted their offer, knowing full well that's where it ended; I was not going to give any details or seem unable to cope. I had my counsellor. I also had my friend, Shirley K (as I would call her); of course, I knew I had God.

Shirley listened to me raging, laughed with me, and always maintained a supportive presence. Her honesty and straight talk infuriated me and cushioned me. We prayed together, disobeyed our head teacher, and confided in each other. Shirley never made judgements about my husband, and I never made judgements about her husband. She was always my best friend.

My family were my staunchest supporters. I thank God always for my family. They were by no means faultless. As my friend Sammy often said, "You all are very clannish." At times, we were indeed clannish, which became our strength and weakness.

Chapter 35

The Years In-Between

My husband had left and moved out, but as mentioned earlier, he still came every morning, took the children to school, and picked them up after school. He paid the mortgage on the house, helped with the bills, and mowed the lawn. He repeatedly said, "I just do not sleep here." He even came and took us to church on Sabbaths.

I let him have his cake and eat it. Days and months went by, and we still engaged in this unreal experience of marriage. Gradually, we became intimate again. It might not have been my brightest decision; I sometimes regretted it and ignored him, but this would last only a few weeks. It seemed as if we could not live with each other, but neither could we live without each other.

I started praying more earnestly, seeking the help I often spoke so eloquently about without experiencing it. My walk with God was erratic and theoretical at its best. In the meantime, the emotional roller-coaster kept going, even while it went nowhere.

It was 1995 when the Soufriere Hills volcano erupted, and we had to move. My husband came to get us. I remember the hysteria and fear of that fateful morning as the mountain rocked and blazed with fire. It was the start of the summer holidays, and my sons were out with their cousin to take care of the animals in Riley's when I heard the rumble and the screaming. My daughter was getting dressed for Vacation Bible School, and my three-year-old son was in the shower. I ran to the window, and my heart froze with fear.

Frantically, my eyes searched for the mountain path where they were. I picked up the phone, and I called their dad. He was on his way. I hurriedly dressed my son. I saw the twins running down the mountain track, my mother struggling to keep up with them. I prayed. They reached home, gripped with fear. Minutes after the boys arrived, their dad was there. Everything happened so fast. He just took charge. He found a place for us to stay through his company, so he moved us. We were living together again. It was as if we were not separated at all.

Every day, he arrived home for lunch with his closest friend. It seemed as if the rift was mended, but it was not. As soon as we moved back to our home and the danger from the volcano was averted, things were back to what they were before that evacuation.

We settled into a pattern. He demanded that I keep away from other men. He would turn up at odd times to ensure I had no man in his house. I was sometimes defiant, sitting on the phone talking to an old friend late into the night to avert my loneliness and fear of the future, until one thoughtless friendship landed me in hot water. I thank God for his grace and mercy as He intervened, and as embarrassing as it was, I was saved from making a complete fool of myself.

After that incident, I better understood how easy it is to become involved in relationships that fill the need for validation and self-worth. It is never any good to allow other men or women who do not hold the same values you have to become your confidante or even just a sounding board. It is never any good to share your fears and anxieties with people of the opposite sex when you are experiencing the trauma of a failing marriage.

I fully understand the adage, "Show me your company, and I will tell you who you are." My mother used to say that to us as we grew up whenever she did not approve of some friend we had taken up with. Friends must be chosen for the value they can add to your life, especially when you are at a low ebb in your life. Too often, these friends turn out to be opportunists bent on satisfying their egos, irrespective of the fragility of their victim. Village life should have taught me. I was to blame. Life on a treadmill is exhausting and filled with potholes.

My husband would come every Sunday to take our young son to the airport to watch the planes come in. He loved airplanes and usually looked eagerly at the door for his dad, but as soon as the aircraft were out of sight, he only wanted to come home to me. My children were the joy of my life. He would take the children out sometimes, and they would visit him.

Sometimes, their dad would try to talk to act as if all was well, but the resentment was ever present, so we would still argue, and I would tell him not to come back to the house again. He was presently engaged in one of his affairs, and I was angry. One Sunday morning, things exploded like I had never dreamed of. Both my friend Shirley K and our pastor's wife repeatedly suggested that I should try not to chase him away. They thought that we could mend our relationship. A group of us women in troubled marriages and relationships had come together. We used to go to the beach on Sunday mornings with the pastor's wife to pray and talk. The pastor's wife wanted us to support and encourage each other and overcome our disappointment and bitterness. I was learning to take time for myself to relax and try to make friends.

The pastor's wife was a lovely woman, always a source of encouragement. We had spoken that morning before my husband came. It was odd for him to turn up, but I thought little of it. The pastor's wife called to check that I was alright. When I wondered why, she laughingly said she only thought of me. We laughed together, and I hung up the phone.

I still found it strange until I discovered my errant husband had gone to the airport to see off his current girlfriend. The pastor's wife had seen them at the airport, and knowing I would soon hear from some busybody, she wanted to come and pick me up, but I had told her I was fine as, at that point, I had no idea what had occurred. By the time I found out, I just went into high gear.

Just as I got off the phone with the individual who broke the news, my dear husband drove up simultaneously. I picked up a stone and threw it into his car windscreen. He struck me so hard that I ended up in the hospital, unable to see out of my left eye. He had never once before in all our arguments ever tried to be physically abusive. I decided this was the end.

I refused to see him or speak to him. He pleaded with my friend to see if I would relent, but I declined. I felt this was it. No more! He was pretty horrified at the fact that he had hit me. My father went after him. Dear Dada. Lovingly protective. My husband kept coming to the hospital, and I had nothing to say to him. He wept and apologized. I held on to my disappointment, anger, and disgust. I tried to pray, but too much hate continually flowed into my mind, and all I kept telling God was that I did not deserve this.

I stopped talking to God and felt it was time to leave this furnace. Yet even this, we were able to get past. My eye had been temporarily damaged. Only God alone had saved it. Despite my refusal to talk to God, He had restored it. He let me rage in my anger and disappointment, doing what only God does, giving me room to scream in bitter silence. My sight returned entirely in a few days. God is good. Years have passed, and I still see.

I went off to study English at Cavehill in 1997. We were relocated again that year because of the volcano. Again, my husband came, picked us up, and found a place for us to stay. It was not the best, but we were not in a communal shelter. I arranged with my sister to keep our daughter and left the boys with him.

We lived together, and he tried to do better. We still argued, but it was not as frequent. That first year at Cavehill was pretty tough for me. I had never been away from my children for so long. I worried constantly about them, but their dad took up the responsibility and did the best he knew how to.

Chapter 36

Parenting From a Distance

One of the many issues that dogged our marriage was our attitudes to discipline and authority. I found it hard to repeat expected standards constantly, and I operated on the idea that children can do as they are told. While corporal punishment was not something I felt was always a go-to, sometimes it was needed. Much of the disciplining of the children was left to me, especially in the years leading up to our separation. I managed the home on my own.

It did not seem to be a problem until I had gone off to university, and my husband was then left with the children. While they were in Montserrat, things were fine, as the extended family was quite valuable for providing wide-ranging support. My daughter could not stand the separation from her brothers, so their dad took her home with him. They were happier being back together, and things were going well. They were fed, clothed, and taken to school and church. Things were fine. They even learned skills that I had felt they were too small to handle. I was wrong. They learned how to wash and iron their own clothes.

When I returned home at the end of the first semester, we were happy to be together. We had long walks in the early mornings and sometimes evenings while our children played with their cousins. It seemed a massive change was on its way. I wanted some money, but to my horror, when I checked my account, my money was practically gone.

When I asked him why, I was given some stories about him spending it on the children. He had stopped paying the mortgage because our home, being in the shadow of a volcanic mountain, was in an unsafe zone. (This I knew about but did not think was justified stopping payment.) In addition, the insurance had not been paid. So, what had he done with the money? We were thrown in a twist. It was stormy. I accused him of lying and spending my money on his affairs. For days, I was silent again. I was convinced I could not...I would not forgive him.

I had to go back to UWI (University of the West Indies), still without any real answers as to when this would end. I laughed, put my mind in gear, and headed off to continue my studies. Eventually, that, too, was swept under the carpet, parked away in the arsenal of my mind, but only to be brought out when he slipped up again. Resentment hurts.

Eventually, after another volcanic eruption, we decided he should take the children to the United Kingdom until I finished university. Then, we would return to Montserrat. Looking back, I know it was one of the most challenging decisions I had to make. I wept as he left with the children while I was left behind in Barbados. I struggled to sleep at night, worried about what might be happening to my children.

I missed him. I kept the shirt he had changed from that last day in Antigua, and it had not been washed for months. Having it near was how I slept when I was too worried, as I could smell him beside me. I knew it was hard for him. I prayed for him, and I called as often as I could.

Soon, the children were enrolled in school. They were fine. I flew to England at the end of every semester. In Barbados at UWI, I would cook on Sundays, package my food for the rest of the week, and save to buy my ticket to the UK.

Things were looking up. I wrote long letters to him—letters I still have. Writing was not his strength, and I accepted that. I knew something was wrong when he started calling me to complain about the children. I was in Barbados, and he was in the UK, yet I had to sort and fix every problem. Somehow, I knew there was a woman involved again, but when I asked, he denied it. I wanted to believe him, so I did.

When I came to England one summer, he took me shopping weekly. We stopped by a friend's house (so he described it) to pick her up and take her shopping. I was unknowingly walking and talking with the woman my husband was sleeping with. It was her brother who told me the truth. The audacious dishonesty was too much. I just went quiet. Little did he realize it was his blatant affairs that fostered the disrespect of our children towards him.

Returning to Barbados, I managed the children's behaviour remotely. We understood each other; they understood my every look and the nuances in my voice. I was their mother. I would laugh with them, and sometimes we played board games together, but I was not their friend; I was their parent. We had spent those years together when I had no friends and went to work, shop, and church. When they went to bed at night, I read until I fell asleep, that is, whenever I was not speaking to Shirley or Sammy on the phone. These two were my constant companions. I did not cry when they were around; I just kept going. I finally finished university and moved to England. By this time, we somehow knew we could not return to Montserrat.

Chapter 37

A New Beginning?

O nce again, without saying it, we just decided we would give our marriage another chance. However, he said it seemed we lived better when we were apart. He was again in a community club. I attended a few times but became bored, so I stopped. Then, the accusations came again. They sounded like, "You need to learn to make friends. I am just your husband, not your friend. I cannot take you anywhere; you are always cold to my friends."

There was no point in trying to reason. I still wanted to believe that he was not having an affair. We merely coexisted. I kept quiet while he held to his mantra: "We have to communicate." I would retort: "I cannot speak to you. It is like speaking to a wall. You do not listen. You do not reason." Both of us were right.

He kept going to his clubs and spending night after night visiting friends who did not act superior to him. I just kept quiet. At times, it was as if I had lost all will to work with him. I knew what the answer would be. I would be accused of being unfriendly.

I knew nothing was left, so I looked after my children, went to work, and went to church. I taught Sabbath class. I went to prayer meetings and the Advent Youth Society. I prayed and hoped God heard. I know He did. Often, I did not feel or accept His presence like the girl who grew up in the Village. Religion was put on and taken off at will like a garment.

I felt better when I knew God was there. When I became angry and frustrated, I would walk early in the morning and plan lessons late into the night. My feelings were often masked under a constant smile, involvement in discussions at church, and otherwise serving in the church. I did all this while still intensely disliking my husband and, equally, the women he was involved with.

The children and I went to church. I tried to keep them involved in church activities. The two younger ones attended Pathfinder Club. The twins were now adults. I depended on them a lot. They are good boys. I know that sometimes it must have been hard for them. They were never rude, and they did not complain. My greatest desire is that my children will be saved. The Lord knows the example they saw was never what it should have been.

Finding work as a teacher in the UK was not easy. It was a couple of years before I could get a full-time job as an English teacher at the high school my youngest son was attending. By this time, I was also caring for my father, who had been diagnosed with prostate cancer. Again, my husband had moved out. We agreed he would still pay our mortgage and child support for our youngest.

I struggled through the first year, always smiling in public and doing all I could as a mother. Life was tough. The twins had moved to live with my father after a fallout, but even this proved to be God's providence. I was so relieved when they were there with my father at night. I no longer needed to sit with him late into the night to keep him company.

Eventually, my father got worse. He needed care I could not give as I continued to teach full-time. It was hard. Sometimes, I had help from the extended family, and I knew they were there. I never talked much about how I felt. I just kept going. Even at church, I told only one friend, El, about the pain I felt and the loneliness. She was a blessing. Always honest and plain-spoken, she believed in justice and fair play.

El supported my daughter when she had a difficult time at church. This woman of God was perfect in her own sphere. The world needs many more like her. I remember her help and her willingness to listen. Then there was my friend Shirley K. What a woman of God. She would always call when I was finding the way hard. We would talk for hours, and then we would pray. The sense of God's presence and His peace was there when we spoke. She was such a blessing to me.

Chapter 38

Restoration

As my father lay sick, I realized I had to find my way back to God on a more personal level. By now, I had been diagnosed with diabetes and was out of work for a while. My sons helped provide food as I watched my savings depleting and worried. I began to pray more, and then one evening, as I was studying, the thought hit me: How could I seek forgiveness from God when I had not forgiven others who had hurt me and with whom I was angry? God gave me the courage to seek forgiveness. After I did and let go of my hatred and anger, things began to look up.

I was doing well at school, and as I developed as a teacher, my students got better results. I was happier and felt I had now let go of the hurt, and things had begun improving. I started to pray from a heart free of resentment for my husband. When my husband went on a holiday trip and had all his stuff stolen in the hotel, I was the one he called to complain to. We had been getting on better before he left, but he still had not given up on his latest affair. I laughed.

I used to go for walks early in the morning when I struggled to face another lonely day. I cried out to God aloud as I sat under a tree in the park. One morning, as I wept out my anger and my bitterness, I finally asked God to give me His forgiveness. It was as if a shower of rain washed over me. I felt at peace. I no longer felt angry or hurt when I thought about how my husband had treated me.

I felt sorrow for his inability to see how he was destroying himself and the negative ways his continued affairs had impacted his relationship with the children. They did not think much of his opinions and were sometimes disrespectful. He blamed me, and I laughed. Strangely, I could not understand how he did not see that I did not have to say anything. They were right there. They lived the life we had provided for them as parents.

Night after night, I tried to settle the matter in my mind. I had no reason to give him yet another chance. As I again justified my right to end it one morning, a quiet voice reminded me:

God does not treat us like that. Following this, I agreed he could come home. He promised never to leave ever again.

I had to tell my two younger children he was coming back. Our younger son was angry, and I understood why. I was sorry I had been a critical factor in this limiting experience.

So, as I attempted to justify my decision, I spoke of the fact that he was their father, and God allows and wants us to forgive. I reminded him that he cared for them financially, and when he was called for any reason, he often came. He accepted that I had a right to decide, and he would live with my decision. I love my children. It was hard for them to accept, but they did.

Our marriage has been far from plain sailing. It was hard, and we hit many obstacles. Troubles aside, my husband tried his best, but sometimes, a word, an act, or an attitude would put me in a tailspin. I learned how to pray. I learned again and again that forgiveness must be a choice. I learned that God does indeed wash and give us new hearts.

As the months went by, I marvelled at how I could talk freely about something that had impacted me on such a level with no anger or resentment. The past does shape the future. I know that sometimes I did not want to love my husband.

Whenever these seasons threaten to dismantle my peace, I think: *How could I love God unless I love my husband?*

I learned that God does not want us to learn to love; He calls us to love. Just as I chose repeatedly to forgive my husband, I decided repeatedly to love him. It was reciprocal in the end. He, too, had to learn.

Years before, another wise man had said something similar when we were separated for a second time. He told me I should never fight with the man but fight with God. He reasoned that since God joined us and gave him to me, I must let God fix him. It is such a simple solution and so filled with biblical truth.

I reasoned that God did not give him to me the first time, nor did He the second time. I had chosen him, so why should God fix him. Thank God He does not reason like me! The prophet Isaiah writes, "For my thoughts are not your thoughts, neither are your ways my ways, saith the Lord. For as the heavens are higher than the earth, so are my ways." (Isaiah 55:8-9 KJV)

Did I know this biblical principle? Of course, I did. I often repeated it when things were well and whenever I needed to comfort someone else. But at this point in my life, it did not apply. Again, I was reminded how difficult it is to take one's advice. It is strange how we can say the right things to someone else, mouth these beautiful thoughts from the word of God, but then fail to apply them to our circumstances.

Chapter 39

Full Circle

When faced with a broken marriage, broken lives, or what we today label as brokenness, the support of the church brothers and sisters is needed more than ever. There were some older folks in the church who you just knew were praying for you. The elders at Faith were incredible men of wisdom and genuinely cared about our family. I do not have their permission to name them, as all three are now deceased. These men, I know, loved God.

They came, prayed, and gave us advice, individually and together. As he sat on the porch leaning on his stick, one of them reminded me, "You are his wife; do not lose sight of that. It does not matter what the world thinks. If he wants to make love to you, you must not refuse him." I laughed, but he was dead serious.

Another one pointed out I should not rush into a divorce because God hates "putting away." I reminded him I had not sent him anywhere, and he was involved with another woman. He said, "God forgives you, too, and you will need to learn to forgive." He explained he was not suggesting that we had to get back. The reasoning was, if God were to treat us as we deserve, who could stand? Besides, he pointed out, "Just consider the children." I told him God would provide, and he smiled patiently and agreed. I knew years later just what he meant.

Just like the church fathers, there were the church mothers who prayed and smiled, giving their encouragement and support. I remember the pastor's wife, who used to come every Sunday morning to pick me up and take me to the beach, where she had a group of women who were either struggling in unhappy marriages or, like me, had separated from their husbands. To this day, I do not understand how she managed to have the time when she, too, had incredibly young children. I was never good at speaking about personal things to others. I felt my problems were mine and nobody else's, but this lady was special. I loved this godly woman and knew she genuinely cared about us. She never pried. If you felt like speaking, she listened and prayed. What a spirit-filled, lovely woman. She was a blessing to me in those tough times.

Now, I can smile and fully understand that the church is not perfect. I fully believe in the idea that the church is a hospital and that all are sick. I laughed then at the ones who thought I deserved what I got. I do not speak of this out of anger, just with a grateful heart because God is patient with us. I know that I would have been equally critical if I were not in my walk with the Lord. I know this because each time I prayed, I wanted God to punish my husband and all the women who came on the scene. I felt it was only just. After all, I had done nothing to deserve what I got.

I thank God that He showed me I was so misguided. My pride made me believe I was good. The reality is I was far from good. It is only God alone who is good. Growing up in the Village taught me the value of hard work and resilience. It did not teach emotional growth, but it did work for some of us as we remained sane by God's grace. Some carry scars that are so deep they refuse to let them surface. Too many have been hardened this way. While I do not believe in telling your suffering and pain to mere mortals, I believe in the power of God's Word and prayer. Healing comes only from God. Forgiveness is a gift of God. Love is a principle, not an emotion. In 2023, while penning this book, we celebrated forty years of marriage. There has not been a single year, month, day, hour, or minute when God has not been present. We just did not look for Him often enough.

As a child on Oswald Street, I ran and laughed, picked guavas, and rushed to school. We saw our parents work hard, struggling to educate us. It was there that we learned of good neighbours. We lived with good neighbours. As an adult, I took my husband home to Oswald Street, where he built us a house, a shelter all our own. At times, he was so strong. At times, we were so weak.

One day, he left me on Oswald Street, but I was never forgotten. Over many days, weeks, months, and years, he came back when he was needed. It was on Oswald Street where many foundations were laid. Many memories lie buried there on Oswald Street. Today we walk together, just the two of us; the children have chosen their own paths. Today, we pray that they will grow to know the love and peace that only God can supply.

About the Author

Vanesta Lewis is a Birmingham-based writer who has always had a passion for sharing the stories of real people. Growing up in the beautiful Caribbean Island of Montserrat, she was heavily influenced by the Bible, historical fiction, and West Indian culture, which can be seen in her funny and thoughtful representation  of the places and times depicted in *Oswald Street*. In her writing, Vanesta's fascination with real-life stories has led her to focus predominantly on the challenges, successes, and joy of growing up in rural Montserrat, as she believes in the power of sharing the challenges and strength of everyday individuals.

Vanesta's writing seeks to illuminate the untold stories and resilient spirits of those who have faced adversity. She hopes that through her work, she can bring understanding, empathy, and connection to readers from all walks of life.

When she's not crafting compelling narratives, Vanesta indulges in her hobbies, which include reading, cooking up new recipes, and getting involved in community projects. She finds inspiration in the diverse community around her and firmly believes in giving back.

Printed in Great Britain
by Amazon

48324060R00106